Christmas Cookies
Are for Giving

Recipes, Stories, and Tips for Making Heartwarming Gifts

Christmas Cookies Are for Giving

Recipes, Stories, and Tips for Making Heartwarming Gifts

By Kristin Johnson and Mimi Cummins

TVR PUBLISHING
FOUNTAIN HILLS, ARIZONA

Tyr Publishing
PO Box 19895
Fountain Hills, AZ 85269-9895
http://www.tyrpublishing.com/
info@tyrpublishing.com

Ordering Information
To order additional copies, contact your local bookstore or see our Web site. Quantity discounts are available.

Printed on acid-free paper.
Printed in Hong Kong.
Book design by Xenocast http://www.xenocast.com/

ISBN 0-9723473-9-9

Publisher's Cataloging-in-Publication Data
(Prepared by The Donohue Group, Inc.)

Johnson, Kristin.
  Christmas cookies are for giving : recipes, stories, and tips for making heartwarming gifts / by Kristin Johnson and Mimi Cummins.
    p. cm.
  Includes index.
  ISBN: 0-9723473-9-9
1. Cookies. 2. Christmas cookery. 3. Holiday cookery. 4. Baking. 5. Gifts. 6. Christmas stories. I. Cummins, Mimi. II. Title.

TX772 .C457 2003
641.8'654--dc21   2002115167

This book is dedicated to our mothers,
Kathy Johnson and Rita Cummins,
because they believed in us

And to our grandmothers, Kay Liebold,
and Evelyn Garchow, who started it all

CONTENTS

Introduction
Our Story: The Spirit of Giving

by Kristin Johnson and Mimi Cummins

W E LIVED NEXT DOOR to each other as girls and share many happy childhood memories.

Like many people, some of our earliest memories surround Christmas cookies. In fact, we've collected stories from several of you, which appear after the original story "The Giving Christmas Cookie" and the delicious recipes. But we wanted to share with you why we wrote this book, and what Christmas cookies mean to us.

For Mimi, Christmas cookies meant going to her grandma's house with her cousins to bake cookies every year. It was a precious family tradition for all of them. They had lots of fun with flour and sugar and frosting, and of course staying up after bedtime and being spoiled in every way by Grandma.

Another Christmas cookie memory surrounds the holidays at Kristin's house, where Mimi, Kristin and her sister Kate went back and forth so many times from the house to the screen porch where the cookies were kept cool that Kristin's mother Kathy had to clean up a "powdered sugar trail." She still laughs about that. And Mimi still fondly remembers Kathy's powdered-sugar dusted Lemon Bars (the recipe is in this book). It was at Kristin's house that Mimi was first introduced to the wonders of the KitchenAid stand mixer, and was taught that you don't have to follow the recipe exactly to make the very best cookies.

Kristin remembers the kitchen of her grandmother's house, the taste of buckeyes that were always kept in the pantry refrigerator, the sound of the Christmas bell she would pull to make music while the cookies baked. She also remembers her kitchen in the house she grew up in next door to Mimi. Many of her happiest memories involve Christmas cooking and cookies in particular.

Mimi didn't really get into baking until her grandmother Evelyn moved in with their family. Grandma was the baker in the family. At 92 years of age, even with hearing aids, a walker on wheels, and trifocals, there was not a lot that Grandma could do anymore. Until Christmas time, that is. The family agreed she saved up all her energy for this one time of the year. In the days before Christmas she could be heard in the kitchen at 5am, the clang and clatter as she searched for all her favorite utensils could act as an auditory beacon for Santa Claus all the way to the North Pole. Suddenly she was rushing around the kitchen, mulling over cookbooks, squinting at index cards on which her own grandmother wrote down some of our family's greatest treasures. This went on all day for days on end. The rest of them were amazed at this great flurry of activity. Mimi, at a youthful 25 years of age, could not keep pace.

There were age-old recipes, such as Yeast Crisps, that we'd never seen in any cookbook. Many of the recipes, including Judy's Pecan Balls, had been handed down by other members of the family. Some of the traditional recipes dated back to before our ancestors immigrated to the United States. You'll find some of these recipes in this book.

Mimi has wonderful memories of creating beautiful cookie plates to give as gifts to guests or hosts at holiday parties. When Mimi had children of her own, she continued the tradition. Baking cookies with her kids is one of her favorite ways to give of her time and attention.

Christmas cookies mean so much to Mimi that she built a Web site,

Christmas-Cookies.com, to share her family's wonderful recipes with the world. Over time, other family members, friends, and site visitors contributed the more than 365 recipes, making the site one of the best places on the Internet to find that special Christmas cookie recipe. The popularity of the Web site inspired the book because it showed how much Christmas cookies mean to people.

In the Johnson family, Kristin and her sister Kate have taken up cookie baking, although their mom has continued to make her famous Nut Roll (the recipe is in this book), and as the family scatters across the country, the idea of having Christmas together is more important than ever. Similarly, Mimi eventually moved to Canada while the rest of her family lives in the U.S. Living far from home gave her much experience in the art of properly shipping a cookie.

Like many of you, we want to stay connected to our loved ones and to our friends and family around the world. Christmas cookies are more than just baked goods. They are a tangible and tasty link to our past, our traditions, and our memories. They are gifts hand-made with love especially for their recipient. They are a great way to say "I care," and we wanted to write a book about giving and sharing Christmas magic and memories. It's important to remember that you can give (and eat) these cookies all year round, and don't have to wait for a special occasion. Christmas gives the occasion of giving a special meaning, but the spirit of love, family and togetherness is a year-round joy.

That was the idea behind the story, "The Giving Christmas Cookie," and the inspiration for asking other people about their family traditions. The time spent in the kitchen laboring with and for loved ones is as much a part of the joy as the songs, gifts and other merry-making.

We want to thank all of you who sent in your stories, which reflect our own childhood experiences—it was touching to see how many people had fond memories of spending holidays with their grandparents.

We'd also like to thank the many food marketing associations that generously donated their recipes for this project. When deciding which recipes to put in the book, we naturally looked to the top-rated recipes at Christmas-Cookies.com. Many of these were donated by anonymous readers, but when researching their true origin, we found that several of them actually originated with a food marketing association. We were not surprised: these people work very hard to develop recipes to showcase their delicious and essential cookie ingredients. When we contacted them for permission to use their recipes, they were very generous, as you will see when you get to the recipe section of this book. Some of them were so enthusiastic about our project that they developed recipes especially for this book. And so we send out a special thanks to the Wisconsin Milk Marketing Board, the Cranberry Marketing Committee, the California Pistachio Commission, the Hazelnut Council, the California Fig Advisory Board, the American Dairy Association, the Cherry Marketing Institute and the California Walnut Commission.

We hand-selected a list of nearly 50 recipes that make perfect cookies, breads, and candies for giving. These recipes combine cherished favorites such as soft Sugar Cookies, zingy Lemon Bars and fancy Springerle with new delights like festive Cranberry Decadent Cookies, to-die-for Easy Triple Chocolate Caramel Brownies, and sophisticated Hazelnut Cappuccino Cookies. Best of all, the recipes come from our families, from professional chefs and from readers just like you. What a great combination!

You'll also find ideas for baking, giving, and shipping Christmas cookie gifts. Make this holiday a beautiful memory and remember, giving Christmas cookies gives back to you. Yummmm!

The Giving
Christmas Cookie

AS I VISITED MY GRANDMOTHER in Parkside Manor, my daughter Amanda and I agreed it lived up to its reputation for a "Clean, Cheerful, Caring Community." The staff kept the rooms clean, bed linens changed, and residents fed, all with a smile. But the rooms smelled of despair beneath the scent of pine wreaths and cinnamon sachets. The residents shuffled, sat or rested, without the energy they once had.

I told Amanda I never want to end up here. It's hard for a girl of 15 to think about her parents getting old, but Amanda smiled with as much good humor as she could muster in this place. She smiled for me, and for my grandmother Edith, who had Alzheimer's and looked at us with a vague expression on roughened features. Grandma had lived in Alaska for many years when Grandpa worked with the airlines, and had become used to harsh climates. Her hazel eyes, which Mama, my daughter and I all had, didn't quite focus.

We might be looking at her unfocused expression in our own home. Parkside Manor, while well-run, had financial problems, because of the rising costs of insurance, Medicare, prescriptions, and a host of other penalties for caring. Grandma was, to our way of thinking, badly off, and yet according to the state, her Alzheimer's wasn't advanced enough. My mother Emma was in the administrator's office arguing that Grandma needed to have special care.

We lived out of town, and because of raising four kids, plus working as a nurse once they were school age, I couldn't get to see Grandma as much as I wanted, and my children barely knew her. But I was the only one who could have her move in with us. My older sister Kate lived in Paris where she and her husband were raising seven children. As for Mama, she visited Grandma every day, but Dad had a heart condition, and Mama, at 60, was already showing signs of age-related health problems. She didn't have the energy to provide Grandma with the care she needed. At least my children and my husband could help me…even if Amanda did look uncomfortable.

I was a nurse, but I knew I couldn't provide the kind of care and attention that Grandma's condition required. Still, I loved her and couldn't just abandon her. I clung to the memories of the way she had once been, so bright, chatting half the night, and singing constantly. She was still a striking woman, with a face that had once been open and curious. My daughter got her height from Grandma, although Grandma's shoulders were now stooped.

Grandma said, "I thought Kate was in Paris."

"Aunt Kate is in Paris," Amanda said.

"No, Kate is here, aren't you, Kate?" With a thin blue-veined hand, Grandma patted the narrow white-sheeted bed beside Grandpa's leather overstuffed armchair. "Tell me about Paris."

Amanda knelt with a smile on her pretty lips. She had the same raw-boned features as Grandma, softened with youth. "Hi, Great-Grandma. I'm jealous of Aunt Kate, getting to live in Paris."

"My, you're a lovely girl. You're Lucy Diaz's girl all right."

I looked at Amanda, whose eyes were those of a trapped animal's. I sent her a message with my eyes: Please, be kind to her.

"So, is there anything you want for Christmas?" Amanda smiled with composure.

"It's not Christmastime." Grandma stared, eyes confused, at the pinecone wreath on the door. "Mama hasn't put up the decorations."

"I'm sure we can find a tree or something for your room." Amanda slowly rose. "Some mistletoe…or something."

"Mistletoe? My husband and I used to kiss under it. Is it Christmas?" Grandma's voice wavered. "Isn't it summer?"

"No, Grandma, it's Christmas."

Grandma glared at me with an anger I'd never seen. "It's summer! I know it's summer! I can feel how hot it is!"

I'd seen Alzheimer's patients before at the hospital, the way the sweetest person could become intolerable as the disease progressed. Still, I was shocked and saddened. This was a new turn for the worse.

Amanda backed toward the door. "I'm going to go get a soda. Anyone want one?"

"I think we could all use one," I said. "I'll treat. Grandma? Do you want anything?"

Grandma didn't respond, and Amanda pulled me out of the room.

MAMA WAS STILL IN THE ADMINISTRATOR'S OFFICE, and the muffled echoes of angry voices indicated that the conversation was not going well. Amanda and I wandered around the cream-colored halls in search of sodas.

"Are they all like her?" Amanda asked.

"Not all of them are confused." I watched two older men playing shuffle-board and arguing about the score. "But yes, in a way they're all like her."

Amanda shrugged, uncomfortable.

"Sorry I dragged you here?" I hugged her.

"I just wish they could be different."

"Maybe…maybe your grandma can persuade them to keep her here."

"Do you think I'm terrible for being uneasy around her?"

"No, honey. You don't know her. But we all love her, and she needs that love more than ever."

Amanda spotted a soda machine and in her haste tripped over the footrest of a solid steel wheelchair in the hall. Amanda stepped back and stammered an apology to the woman in the wheelchair, gaunt but elegant, with skin as clear and flawless as an angel's. I could see strands of curly white-blond hair escaping from a babushka she wore underneath a broad-brimmed red straw hat decorated with a garland of small white flowers. Like Grandma, she shivered in a thick, soft sweater, and her long red skirt covered her legs.

"Look where you're going." The cocoa brown eyes that looked at Amanda were amused. "Can't wait to get away from the old folks, eh?"

Amanda stood with gawky tall grace. "They're having a sale at the mall."

"I love shopping," the woman said.

"Shopping rules," Amanda agreed. "I'm sorry I knocked into you."

"Believe me, dear, you're a welcome distraction." The woman extended a hand. "My name is Elise."

We introduced ourselves and told her about Grandma.

"Oh, yes, I know her. So sweet, but it's a terrible thing to lose one's mind." Elise clenched her fingers together. I noticed the stiffness in her fingers, and the way she looked tired even by the effort of speaking to us. "But then, we all have our burdens."

"You have rheumatoid arthritis?"

I dealt with a variety of illnesses, and could spot a range of symptoms. A pity I couldn't detect Grandma's Alzheimer's. Granddad shielded us from the knowledge until he died.

"Yes, and it's tiring me. I want to talk to you delightful girls some more, if you'll help me to my room."

Amanda pushed the unwieldy wheelchair to Elise's room, filled with poinsettias and lamps with lacy shades. Paintings of fairy-tale medieval castles on the Rhine and the Loire covered the walls. There was one large photo of a young man with outdoorsy good looks. The photo was signed "À ma chère Élise—Jacques Delacroix."

"My husband." Elise smiled. "I met him when I was studying fashion in Paris."

"Paris!" Amanda's eyes looked more alive. "I'd like to go there and open a café."

Elise squeezed her hand. "He was in the French cinema—he later learned the American custom of signing stars' photographs and gave me this one as a playful reminder of our exciting lives. I was making jewelry and he had—"

She stopped and smiled. "You didn't come here to hear about my life."

"We'd love to," I said, enchanted with this woman.

Amanda looked star-struck at the photograph of Elise's husband, who reminded me a bit of Robert Redford or Harrison Ford.

"He's cute," she said.

"He was wonderful." Elise's face softened with the glow of love never absent. "Sit down, please. It's good to have company."

Amanda sat listening to Elise, and asked questions about fashion, Paris, and falling in love with a romantic movie star. Elise learned about my sister Kate and suggested we make a trip as a family to see her.

"Are you all prepared for Christmas?" she asked.

"Mostly," I said.

"It's wonderful that you take the time out of your holiday to visit Edith." Elise looked toward the small, plain bedside table, a contrast to the bed with its lace counterpane, covered with a cozy quilt the color of Elise's hat. "My children blame my illness for my husband's death. They never come to see me."

Amanda gently touched Elise's hand. "That's awful."

I was proud of my daughter's ability to adapt, and to put people at ease.

"I miss them…but mostly I miss my kitchen, and making the Giving Christmas Cookie. The aroma would fill the whole house. My children and grandchildren thought I was a great cook."

"Giving Christmas Cookie?" Amanda looked interested.

"Ah, I'm getting ahead of myself. Not unheard of when you're older. My ancestors in Vienna, Austria had the most delicious vanilla cookie recipe, *Vanillekipferl*. In 1863, the Aichner family opened a *konditorei*, a pastry and candy shop, where the most delicious smells of rugulach and almond crescents and linzer sandwiches—with raspberry jam that stayed on your tongue—made you cry with the joy of being alive, of sitting there among friends and family, artists, musicians…"

She pointed toward the bedside table. "Could one of you please open the drawer by my bedside, please? You'll find an ebony box inside, and it has *Die Konditorei Aichner* inscribed in gold on the lid."

Amanda opened the drawer and brought out a small enameled box that was so black it reflected Amanda's own silhouette when she turned it on its side. The top reminded me of an intricately decorated cake with ribbons of gold, like frosting, running through the gleaming ebony. The gold rivers formed flowers and leaves and vines that framed the words *Die Konditorei Aichner—Familien und Freunde sind willkommen!*

Amanda opened the box and slowly revealed its treasures: several yellowing, thin parchment sheets covered with elegant, round handwriting, most of it English script. The first sheet was illustrated with angels and cookie cutouts. Amanda touched the word *Vanillekipferl*, done in calligraphy.

"That's German for 'Vanilla Crescents,'" Elise said. "My ancestors would keep the ovens going all day and night, because everyone in Vienna loved the vanilla fragrance and the taste they said was like heaven. My mother took that as her signature recipe, and selling them supported our family. But when I moved to Paris, of course it was not wise to speak German after the war, so I spoke French. When I moved to America with Jacques and the children, I was out of the habit of speaking German, so my children never learned it, and they named the cookie the Giving Christmas Cookie, since we gave the cookies every year as gifts. After my husband died and I moved here, I translated the recipe into English to give to my children so they could continue the tradition. But, of course, they weren't interested."

Amanda gazed at the words. "I gained five pounds just reading this."

"It tastes even better," Elise said. "And in my day, we didn't worry so much about food. We ate with our families. Do you eat dinner together?"

"Most nights," I said. "And Amanda's our baker."

"You enjoy making cookies?" Elise smiled at Amanda. "I wish my grandchildren did. I wish I could share my cookie recipe with them, and the other Christmas cookie recipes and family traditions I collected."

I read another paper. "And this looks like a prayer."

"A kitchen prayer," Elise said. "I call it the before Grace prayer. You recite it while baking."

The prayer read:

> "God bless this mixture with the sweetest and tastiest ingredients: joy, faith, family, friendship, love, and health. Let the scent of this holiday offering rise to Heaven and make the angels sing, for the

*happiness of mankind is their feast. Let us taste our blessings with
each bite as we share the company of our loved ones. Amen."*

Amanda grabbed the box and the papers. "Mom, I just had the most
awesome idea."

The starlight in her eyes made me grin, at both the happiness and the
mischief I knew followed that look.

"What's your idea?"

"ABSOLUTELY NOT." The head nurse, with the dietitian, stood in front of
the door to the kitchen. "We have a strict diet here. Many of these people
are lactose-intolerant, or diabetic, or hypoglycemic."

Amanda presented the recipe for them to read. "We could probably
make something from your recipes. You have dairy substitute and sugar
substitutes, don't you?"

"That isn't the point," the head nurse said. "We have a responsibility."

"And you can't risk liability," I said. The head nurse glared at me.

"We won't cause you any trouble," Elise said.

"We're not concerned for us. We care about our residents," the dietitian
said. "We have Christmas cookies, of course, all carefully prepared—"

"I loved baking Christmas cookies."

I turned to see Mama and Grandma walking together. The head nurse, the dietitian, and Elise all did a double take. Elise reached her hand to Grandma, who grasped her hand.

"Remember, Emma?" Grandma waved at Mama. "When…Stephanie was just a little girl. My sugar cookies." She looked at me. "You always licked the bowl. And…Amanda did too."

I enfolded Mama and my daughter in a big hug as Grandma began to cry. "That's right, Great-Grandma," Amanda said.

The dietitian and the head nurse put their heads together and quietly conferred, then stepped away from the kitchen.

"Make your cookies," the head nurse said.

"Thank you," Elise said to her

"There are 89 residents who have no dietary restrictions," said the dietitian. "You'll need help to make enough for all of them. I'll go see if some of the residents and their families want to help."

THE IMMACULATE KITCHEN was the same creamy color as the butter Amanda placed in a bowl, and it smelled comfortingly of ginger, cinnamon, vanilla, and a hint of disinfectant.

Albert van Doren, a 78-year-old Army veteran in a wheelchair because of military shrapnel in his hips, mixed the batter, talking with Amanda about what a pinch meant, and could you have such a thing as too much vanilla. Elise supervised, giving us instructions on how her family made the cookies, telling us how the dough had to be handled with such care because it was so delicate. Mama and Grandma lined the cookie sheets with parchment paper. I placed the cookies on the sheets, and watched the temperature in the oven. Everyone recited Elise's prayer together, over and over, but took breaks in-between to taste the batter, to laugh for perhaps the first time in months.

Mr. van Doren inhaled the scent of the ingredients and reminisced about his mother's cooking and his experiences as a 25-year-old in World War II.

"We boys in Patton's regiment were huddled with our rifles in France on Christmas Eve with the Germans circling around us, and because the world had gone mad I started daydreaming about my Mama's frosted gingerbread cookies and how I wanted to get out of the war alive so I could taste them again. My wife always said that was the one thing she couldn't make better than my mother."

"I remember my aunt's icebox cookies," said a woman who had terminal cancer. "My mother was hopeless at baking, but my aunt brought cookies every year at Christmas."

"I used to love your candy and fudge, Mom, remember?" The woman's daughter squeezed her hand. "Oh, and buckeyes, those little chocolate-covered peanut butter balls. Who was it who made those?"

Christmas cookie memories filled the air along with the scent of vanilla. Outside, voices of men and women that had not been heard in six months echoed with holiday spirit. We formed a joyous chain and passed the trays out to the exit, where the nursing home staff directed everyone to the common room for an impromptu Christmas cookie party.

Everyone proclaimed Elise the queen of the party, and toasted Amanda with eggnog and hot cider. Amanda collected recipes from everyone and wrote down snippets of their childhoods. Residents and their visiting family shared tales of past Christmases, laughed, sang Christmas carols, and several of them danced. One of the residents had a great-grandchild, a one-year-old, on her lap, and Amanda fed the baby a Christmas cookie. The nursing home staff told me they had never seen the residents more alive and filled with the holiday spirit, and in many ways, they seemed to be a family.

Mama told me about the night I was born. Grandma told Mama about how she'd sung to Mama the minute Mama lay in her arms for the first time. I tried to tell Amanda about her father holding her because I was exhausted, but Amanda covered her ears. In every way, she was a typical teenager. I was just so proud of her and the giving spirit she'd shown. She was growing up, and it thrilled yet saddened me.

While everyone ate the cookies and reminisced, Elise yawned and seemed to have trouble staying awake. Amanda and I accompanied her back to her room, and gave her back the box, which we'd kept during the party so she could enjoy herself. Elise shook her head and gave it back to us.

"My family will never understand its secrets," she said. "I want you to have it. You are a wonderful, loving family. Just please promise to make these cookies every year."

We embraced her, giving her an extra hug and kiss on behalf of Mama, who had chosen to talk to the administrator and Grandma. The administrator told Mama that Grandma was a gentle person and liked by the staff and several of the residents. "What are we here for, if we can't give your mother the care she needs?"

We suggested that we take Grandma home for a visit just before Christmas, and I volunteered to take her to Christmas Eve dinner in the town. We went back to see Elise and asked her if she would like to come with us. Elise smiled and said no. "Edith deserves all your attention."

ON CHRISTMAS EVE DAY, the residents and staff of Parkside Manor waved and smiled in greeting to me and to my daughter as we walked through the hallways to Grandma's room. We discovered that Grandma had packed, and she stood up to hug us.

"We have to say hello to Elise," Amanda said. "I just had another awesome idea. Maybe we could change her mind."

"She's gone home." Grandma had tears in her eyes. "I never said goodbye to her."

Amanda gasped. "She didn't have anyone…"

"Her family took her home." Grandma grabbed Amanda's hand. Amanda held her comfortingly until one of the nurses, a thin-faced woman with a kind smile, came. I took her aside.

"What happened to Elise Delacroix?"

The nurse looked sympathetic but professional. "You were here, that night, with the cookies."

"Yes." I stared at her. "That night—?"

The nurse nodded. "She died in her sleep."

Amanda just stood in shock. I didn't know what to say.

The nurse saw our distress, and placed a comforting hand on my shoulder. "The people here haven't stopped talking about you and your daughter. They were telling Elise's family—"

Amanda reached out, her arm trembling, and the nurse steadied her as she stumbled. I felt my own tears, and the nurse held both of us in a way that didn't intrude, but comforted instead.

"Her family…" I couldn't speak. "She said they…"

The nurse walked between us, waving us onward. We followed as if in a trance.

"Are they here?"

"This morning."

"We should say something to them." I felt numb. "She was such a lovely lady."

"They want to talk to you," the nurse said.

The nurse navigated the corridors, stopping to clasp the hands of the people reaching for her. At least half a dozen people embraced us. I kept talking to the nurse, who seemed to understand my need to chatter on. She told me that Elise's children had come to make funeral arrangements. They had already taken away her belongings from storage, and had been questioning all the residents about Elise.

"Why do they want to talk to us?" I asked.

The nurse smiled. "Maybe to thank you for being so kind to her?"

Amanda put her face in my shoulder. "Oh, Mom…"

I stroked her hair, and saw ahead of us, near the administrator's office, a hard-faced man and woman standing on either side of the head nurse, slowly moving in a circle around her whenever she tried to step away from them. The nurse prodded us forward. The head nurse saw us and nodded wordlessly at Amanda and me. The hard-faced man and woman turned and stepped forward in tandem. I extended my hand in a handshake. The woman's attractive features definitely resembled Elise's. The man was husky, with his father's features and his mother's eyes. They didn't take my hand.

"You're Elise's children." I lowered my hand and shifted my feet awkwardly.

They introduced themselves, more out of surprise than any warmth. I wanted to think they were shattered by their mother's death.

"I'm so sorry about your mother," I said.

"Don't be," the woman said.

"Thank you," the man said, out of politeness. "But it was for the best."

Amanda stared at them, tears pouring down her cheeks, and then sobbed into my shoulder.

"You'd think it was her mother," the woman said to me, then to Amanda: "Get a grip."

Amanda glared at her. I restrained Amanda with a hand. "Amanda is upset by your mother's death."

"We're the ones who have lost her." The woman showed no emotion. "I suppose you think you're entitled to her things too."

"Ask them about the box." The man, goaded by his sister's rudeness, stepped forward. "Ask them."

"You were at their little geriatric party," the woman said. "You must have seen the box. It's a black box—an antique. We deserve it."

"Are you going to make the Christmas cookie?" Amanda asked.

"That stupid waste of time?" The woman snorted. "We buy all our Christmas cookies. Who has time to cook?"

"We're her children so we get everything of hers," the man added.

"We didn't find any box," the head nurse said.

The woman grabbed Amanda and pulled her forward. "We've questioned everyone and they don't have the box. You were the last people with her before she died, so you must have it. Give it to us!"

I thought of the way they acted and understood why Elise didn't want them to have the box. They were her children, but still…Amanda had shown more warmth and interest in Elise than these two. Amanda kept the box in her room, studying its recipes and its traditions. Sometimes when I would look in on her I would see her smiling, staring into the distance for a moment, and I could feel Elise's presence. It was odd, because I'd only met the woman once, but there was no doubt she had become a special person in our lives.

Amanda looked at me, and I knew she was asking me if we had to give the box back. Elise's daughter noticed and advanced on me. "Where is it? You stole it!"

The head nurse blocked her way. "I realize you're grieving, but this is highly inappropriate."

"You're supposed to be on our side." The woman turned on her. "After all we paid to put Mom in this dump—"

The head nurse remained calm. "I believe we have some more formalities to complete. If you want to file a complaint about us, you of course are free to do so. If you'll step into the administrator's office—"

Amanda took the man's hand, with a grace that stole my breath right from my chest. "I'm really sorry about your mom." She nodded at the woman, who turned around and marched into the office.

The man let his hand linger in Amanda's for a moment, then flushed and muttered a goodbye. He followed his sister into the office.

"If they file a complaint, I doubt anyone will listen," the head nurse said. "We keep a record of visitors. This is the first time they've come here since they deposited her at Parkside Manor."

"It makes me feel bad that they never understood how important baking the Giving Christmas Cookie was, and how important spending time with Elise was," Amanda said. "Thanks for helping us out."

The head nurse squeezed my daughter's hand. "No. Thank you. Will you come and make those cookies every year for our annual Christmas

Cookie Social?"

I smiled at what my daughter had started. "We'd love to."

Amanda sobbed, and I put my arm around her as we walked.

"Merry Christmas to you and your grandmother," the head nurse said.

"What was that about your awesome idea, Amanda?" I asked as we took Grandma to the car.

Amanda was quiet.

"Amanda?" I gentled my voice. "I'm really proud of you and the way you come up with ideas to help people."

Amanda gulped back tears. "Oh…I was thinking maybe we could make a book of all those great recipes and stories, with the Giving Christmas Cookie recipe in the front, and the prayer too. And we could give it as a present to all those people."

Then, she burst into tears. Grandma, who sat in the back with her, patted her hand and held her gently. I fought my tears until I could cry with my daughter at home.

A YEAR LATER, Grandma presented the *Christmas Cookie Book of Giving* at the Parkside Manor Christmas Cookie Social. She wore a hat for what Mama said was the first time in years. It was a pink broad-brimmed ladies' hat, and she had it on backwards with the ribbon in the back. Amanda adjusted it when Grandma was occupied talking to Mr. Van Doren and his grandson Adam, a tall high school boy and track champion who lived in the town and kept grinning at Amanda and bringing her glasses of punch.

The baby Amanda had held the year before was now running around the room trying to crawl on everyone's laps, and the two men who the year before had argued cantankerously about shuffleboard now took turns playing "horse," bouncing him on their knees. There was even a Santa Claus, a cancer patient who laughed harder than anyone else, and a Mrs. Claus, a former dancer whose ankles swelled from pain.

Grandma gave the Santa Claus and Mrs. Claus a box full of copies of the book, which Amanda did on her computer and took to the printer's the month before. As Grandma presented the book, the residents all applauded and passed around the trays of the Giving Christmas Cookie that the staff, Mama and I kept bringing out of the kitchen.

I felt certain Elise was in the room with us, embracing us all…and then reaching for one of her Christmas cookies.

Christmas Cookie Baking:
Tips and Hints

Christmas Cookie Baking: Tips and Hints

W E MAKE HOME-MADE COOKIES for lots of reasons. Sometimes it's because they remind us of our grandmothers and days gone by. Often, it's because we want some quality time with our kids. Or it's to re-live or hand down a family tradition. And of course, because home-made cookies taste better. Whatever your reasons for baking, you want the results to be delicious, and you want the process to be a relaxing and fun experience. It's all too easy to get caught up in the holiday rush and stress even when baking cookies, so here are some reminders, tips, and hints to help your baking go smoothly and yield the best results.

Be Prepared

- Schedule baking cookies so that you're not rushed or distracted by holiday preparations, family, or last-minute chores.

- The first thing you should always do when baking cookies is to read your recipe all the way through. Ideally, you should do this at least a few hours before you plan to do your baking, so that you have time to go out and buy any ingredients you need and do any preliminary steps such as taking the butter out of the refrigerator to soften.

🍃 Before you start baking, make sure you have all the necessary ingredients and tools at hand. Take out everything you will need and place it on the counter. This way you won't find that you lack something critical when you've got the batter half-made.

🍃 Ingredients must be at the proper temperature. You may be ready to make your cookies right now, but if the recipe calls for softened butter and yours is still rock-hard in the refrigerator, your cookies will not turn out right.

🍃 If the ingredient list calls for chopped nuts or lemon zest (the colored part of the peel, without the white pith), chop your nuts and zest your lemon before you start to put together the rest of the ingredients. The same goes for anything that you need to grate, slice, or otherwise manipulate before the ingredients get assembled.

🍃 Don't forget to pre-heat your oven if the recipe calls for it. Cookies will not bake correctly if the oven isn't at the right temperature when they go in. The best thing to do is to turn on the oven first, then start making the batter. By the time the batter is done the oven will be ready.

🍃 If you have many different kinds of cookies to bake in one day, set out all your ingredients on the counter and make each type of dough assembly-line fashion, one dough recipe after another. Wrap each dough ball in plastic wrap and put it in the refrigerator, then start on the next recipe. When all the dough is made, put away your ingredients, clean up the kitchen, and start baking all the different kinds of cookies. This saves you time, energy, and space.

The Right Ingredients

🕊 Your cookies will only be as good as the ingredients you put into them.

🕊 Use fresh ingredients. Stale ingredients can impart their flavors and odors to your cookies and you will be disappointed in the outcome. Do not use nuts, flour, chocolate, or anything else that is past its prime. You'll know it's past its prime if you've had it in the cupboard since last Christmas or it smells funny.

🕊 Baking powder and baking soda also need to be fresh. They don't go stale, but they lose their effectiveness after a few months. Test baking powder by mixing 1 teaspoon (5 ml) with ½ cup (125 ml) hot water, or baking soda by mixing ¼ teaspoon (1 ml) with 2 teaspoons (10 ml) vinegar. In either case, the mixture should bubble immediately. If it doesn't, then it needs to be replaced.

🕊 Use quality ingredients. If you use quality chocolate, real butter, and genuine vanilla extract, your cookies are always going to taste better than if you use generic chocolate, margarine or butter-flavored shortening, and artificial vanilla. You really can taste the difference. However, use shortening or margarine if the recipe specifically calls for it because this will have an effect on the texture of the cookie.

The Right Tools

🕊 Use an oven thermometer to make sure that your oven temperature is accurate.

❯ If you're baking a lot of cookies, a heavy-duty stand mixer will make things go much easier and quicker than using a hand-held. Plus, a stand mixer will last years longer than the less durable hand-helds.

❯ Invest in a couple of quality insulated cookie sheets to prevent your cookies from burning on the bottom. We find that the darker colored non-stick variety make cookies brown too quickly, so we prefer to use a silver-colored sheet with parchment paper or one of the popular non-stick baking mats. Either way, your cookie sheet should not have raised edges, since that prevents an even flow of heat around the cookies.

❯ If you're making bar cookies, use the correct size pan. If the pan you are using is a different size than the one specified in the recipe, your cookie may not turn out and at the very least you will have to adjust your baking time.

❯ Get a good cookie press for making Spritz, a real Springerle roller for making Springerle, and a nice assortment of interesting cookie cutters. Simple, inexpensive tools like these will turn out cookies with a professional look that will impress the recipients of your gift.

The Right Technique

❯ Measure ingredients accurately. To measure dry ingredients, use graduated measuring cups in ¼-cup, ⅓-cup, ½-cup, and 1-cup sizes. Lightly spoon the ingredient into the appropriate cup until it heaps over. Take the blunt, straight edge of a knife and sweep the extra off the top to level off the contents of the cup. Do not pack the ingredient into the cup unless you're measuring brown sugar.

🍂 If an ingredient is supposed to be chopped or diced, pay attention to whether it's measured before or after chopping. If the recipe calls for "1 cup of walnuts, chopped" that means that you are supposed to measure one cup of walnuts and then chop them. "1 cup of chopped walnuts" means that you chop them first and then measure out 1 cup.

🍂 To measure wet ingredients, use a 2 or 4-cup glass measuring cup marked with graduated measurements. Fill up the cup to the line indicating the appropriate measurement. Make sure to check the measurement at eye level. Don't look down at it or an optical illusion may prevent you from adding the correct amount. If you are measuring something sticky such as honey or molasses, grease the cup first and then it will slide out easily without sticking to the cup.

🍂 Butter, shortening, and margarine should have the measuring amounts marked on the side of the package. If they don't, or if you're trying to measure something like peanut butter, you can fill a 2-cup measure with 1 cup of cold water and then add the ingredient until the measure reaches 1 cup plus the amount that you need. For example, if you need ½ cup of peanut butter, add peanut butter to the 1 cup of water until the measure reaches 1½ cups. You will then have 1 cup of water plus ½ cup of peanut butter. Pour out the water and then add your ingredient as the recipe states.

🍂 When adding large chunks such as chocolate chips or nuts, make sure that they are distributed evenly throughout the dough.

🍂 Learn how to roll out your dough without using too much flour or over-handling it, which can make your sugar cookies and gingerbread cookies turn out dry and tough. Rolling the dough out between two sheets of waxed paper or plastic wrap can help with this. If the dough is very sticky, you may want to use the waxed paper with a little bit of flour. After you cut out your cookies, save the trimmings and re-roll them all at once. Don't keep adding the trimmings to the dough you haven't rolled yet.

❧ Using a cookie press can take practice. You can put your mistakes back into the press and try again.

❧ Always make your cookies the same size, shape, and thickness, and space them evenly, so that they will bake uniformly.

❧ When baking drop cookies, put your cookies 2 inches apart on the cookie sheet to allow room for spreading. Otherwise you may end up with one giant cookie.

❧ When you bake your second batch, never put the dough on a hot cookie sheet. This will make your cookies spread. Use a cool cookie sheet every time. Ideally you should have three cookie sheets so you can have one in the oven, one cooling, and one to put the next batch of cookies on. If you only have one, run it under cold water and then dry it before using it again.

❧ You can bake two batches of cookies in the oven at the same time if you place one sheet in the middle of the oven and one in the top third. For even baking, switch places halfway through the baking time.

❧ When you remove the cookies from the oven, let them cool on the pan for about 1 minute, and then using a spatula remove them to a wire rack to cool completely. If your cookie starts to fall apart as you take it from the cookie sheet, let it cool a little longer.

❧ Cool your cookies completely before storing them. If you store them while they're still warm, they could get soggy.

❧ If you prefer soft and chewy cookies, try under-baking them by just a minute or two.

Storing Cookies

❧ When you make cookies, it is not always necessary to bake them right away. Most doughs for drop cookies, rolled-out cookies, or refrigerator cookies can be frozen for months before you bake them. Make your dough ahead of time and freeze it wrapped in plastic wrap and placed in a resealable plastic freezer bag. When you're ready to bake, remove the dough from the freezer and thaw it at room temperature, leaving it inside the plastic bag until completely thawed. Bake and decorate as the recipe instructs. Planning ahead this way will allow you the time to bake your cookies so that they come out to your satisfaction.

❧ Batter that is liquid in consistency and can be poured (such as the batter for many bar cookies of cake-like consistency) cannot be frozen.

❧ You can also place your drop cookies, cutouts, or sliced cookies on a baking sheet as if you were going to bake them and then put them in the freezer instead. Once they are frozen solid, remove them from the cookie sheet, store them in an airtight container, and return them to the freezer. When you want to bake an eclectic batch of cookies, just take out the pieces that you need, place them on a baking sheet and pop them into a pre-heated oven. They will need to bake just a couple minutes longer than what the recipe calls for.

❧ Almost any kind of cookie, including bar cookies, can be frozen after baking as long as they aren't decorated with icing or chocolate. Let them cool completely before freezing them, and be sure to store them in an airtight container so that they don't dry out or pick up odors from the freezer. You can decorate cookies once defrosted and before serving them, if you like.

❧ Refrigerated cookies should also be stored in airtight containers so as not to pick up the odors of your refrigerator.

❧ Whether you store them in the freezer, the refrigerator, or at room temperature, different types of cookies should never be stored in the same container. The flavors and odors will transfer from one type to the other, and crisp cookies will soften if stored with chewy ones.

❧ Cookies intended for shipping as gifts require special packaging. See our section on shipping cookies (page 145) for more helpful hints.

Christmas Cookie Recipes

The Giving Christmas Cookie (Vanillekipferl)

The Giving Christmas Cookie (Vanillekipferl)

This traditional Austrian Christmas cookie from our story is laced with the flavor of real vanilla. Delicate and buttery, it truly melts in your mouth. Simple, yet elegant.

⅔ cup (150 ml) sliced blanched almonds

⅓ cup (75 ml) granulated sugar

1 cup (250 ml) unsalted butter, softened

1 teaspoon (5 ml) vanilla extract

1⅔ cup (400 ml) plus 2 tablespoons (30 ml) all-purpose flour

¼ teaspoon (1 ml) salt

½ cup (125 ml) superfine vanilla sugar (see below), or superfine sugar

Place the almonds in a food processor and grind very finely. In a mixing bowl, combine the almonds, butter, sugar, and vanilla and beat until light and fluffy. Stir in the flour and salt until incorporated. Wrap the dough in plastic wrap and refrigerate for 2 hours.

Pre-heat oven to 325°F (170°C). Divide the dough into 6 portions and work with one portion at a time while you keep the rest in the refrigerator. Lightly flour your hands and pinch off enough dough to make a 1-inch (2.5 cm) ball. Knead it for a few seconds to soften it slightly, then form it into a crescent shape and place on an ungreased baking sheet. If you have trouble with the dough becoming too soft while forming the crescents, run your hands under cold water to cool them off after forming every 3 to 4 cookies.

Bake for 12-14 minutes or until the bottoms of the cookies are just starting to take on a golden color. Cool cookies for about 7 minutes on the baking sheet and then roll gently in superfine vanilla sugar while still warm. Allow to cool completely on a wire rack.

Store in an airtight container at room temperature for up to 1 month. Makes about 48 cookies. Because they are so fragile, these cookies are best to give by hand delivery.

Note: To make vanilla sugar, fill a quart (1 *l*) jar halfway up with sugar (in the case of this recipe, use superfine sugar). Then, cut a whole vanilla bean into 1-inch (2.5 cm) pieces and place them in the jar. Fill the jar with more sugar until it is about ⅔ full. Cover it tightly and shake the jar to evenly distribute the vanilla throughout the sugar. Set the jar in a cool dark place for 1 to 3 weeks. The sugar will take on the flavor of vanilla. When you are ready to use the sugar, empty the jar through a sieve in order to separate the vanilla from the sugar. You may re-use the same vanilla pieces several times before they begin to lose their effectiveness.

Cranberry Decadent Cookies

Cranberry Decadent Cookies

Dried cranberries and cinnamon transform this reverse chocolate chip cookie into a holiday favorite. The coffee granules subtly enhance the flavor of the chocolate.

2 cups (500 ml) all-purpose flour

½ cup (125 ml) Dutch process cocoa powder

1 teaspoon (5 ml) ground cinnamon

½ teaspoon (2 ml) baking powder

½ teaspoon (2 ml) baking soda

½ cup (125 ml) unsalted butter, softened

½ cup (125 ml) solid vegetable shortening, softened

½ cup (125 ml) granulated sugar

1 cup (250 ml) light brown sugar, firmly packed

2 large eggs

1 teaspoon (5 ml) vanilla extract

1 teaspoon (5 ml) instant coffee granules

1 cup (250 ml) white chocolate chips

1 cup (250 ml) semi-sweet chocolate chips

1 cup (250 ml) dried cranberries

Pre-heat oven to 350°F (180°C). Grease two baking sheets or line them with parchment paper. Sift together flour, cocoa powder, ground cinnamon, baking powder and baking soda, and set aside.

In a large bowl beat butter, shortening, granulated sugar and brown sugar until light and fluffy. Add eggs, one at a time, mixing until fully combined before additions. In a small cup, mix together the vanilla and the coffee until the coffee is dissolved, then add to the butter mixture; beat to combine. Gradually add dry ingredients, mixing until combined. Stir in white chocolate chips, semi-sweet chocolate chips, and dried cranberries.

Drop 1 tablespoon (15 ml) of dough at a time onto baking sheets, spacing cookies about 2 inches (5 cm) apart. Bake for 8 to 10 minutes or until firm. Let cool for 1 minute then transfer to a wire rack to cool completely.

Store in airtight containers at room temperature for up to 1 month. Makes about 48 cookies. These cookies are excellent for shipping.

photo courtesy of the Hazelnut Council

Hazelnut Cappuccino Cookies

This recipe came to me courtesy of the Hazelnut Council. It has a crispy shortbread texture and a wonderfully sophisticated, modern taste. It's the perfect gift for the gourmet coffee connoisseur.

1½ cup (375 ml) hazelnuts, toasted, skin removed

1¾ cup (425 ml) all-purpose flour

¼ teaspoon (1 ml) salt

1 cup (250 ml) butter, softened

½ cup (125 ml) granulated sugar

½ cup (125 ml) brown sugar, firmly packed

1 tablespoon (15 ml) instant coffee granules

¼ cup (60 ml) semi-sweet chocolate morsels

Pre-heat oven to 325°F (170°C). Place hazelnuts in a food processor. Process until finely chopped, set aside. Sift flour and salt together, set aside. In a large bowl, beat together butter, granulated sugar, brown sugar, and instant coffee granules. Stir in flour mixture and hazelnuts until blended. Shape dough into 1-inch (2.5 cm) balls and place on an ungreased baking sheet. Flatten dough to ¼ inch to ½ inch (0.5 cm to 1 cm) with bottom of glass. If glass starts to stick to dough, dip bottom of glass in granulated sugar.

Bake for 16 to 18 minutes or until golden. Remove from oven and allow to cool 2 minutes on baking sheet, then remove to wire racks to cool completely.

Place chocolate morsels in a small microwaveable bowl. Microwave on high 30 to 90 seconds, stirring every 30 seconds, until melted. Place melted chocolate in a small resealable plastic bag, then snip off a very small corner of the bag. Drizzle chocolate over cooled cookies; allow chocolate to set until firm.

Store in airtight containers at room temperature for up to 3 weeks. Makes about 30 cookies. These cookies ship well if packed carefully.

Note: To remove skin from hazelnuts, toast them in a 350°F (180°C) oven for 15 minutes. Remove from oven and while still hot, place the nuts in a rough dish towel, then rub them briskly with the towel. Most of the skin will easily flake off; it's OK to leave the rest.

Emma Liebold's Date Pinwheels

Emma Liebold's Date Pinwheels

It was always a Christmas tradition as neighbors for Mimi, Kate and I to enjoy recipes from my grandmothers, Kay Liebold and Hannah-Barbara Johnson, and from my great-grandmother Emma Liebold. The warmth of family memories complements the sweet richness of the dates. Emma Liebold passed down her recipes to her family, and her love of writing to me. It's fitting that this recipe should be in the book, because now we have the perfect fusion of family recipes and storytelling traditions. —Kristin

for the filling:

2½ cups (625 ml) chopped dates

2 cups (500 ml) brown sugar

1 cup (250 ml) water

1 cup (250 ml) chopped nuts

for the dough:

1 cup (250 ml) solid vegetable shortening or unsalted butter

1 cup (250 ml) powdered sugar or granulated sugar

3 large eggs, well beaten

4 cups (1 *l*) all-purpose flour

½ teaspoon (2 ml) salt

½ teaspoon (2 ml) baking powder

For the filling, combine dates, sugar and water in a small saucepan, bring to boiling over medium-high heat, stirring constantly. Reduce heat to medium-low, cook 10 to 15 minutes or until thickened, stirring occasionally. Remove from heat and stir in nuts. Set aside.

For the dough, beat shortening or butter and sugar until light and fluffy. Beat in eggs. In a separate bowl, stir together flour, salt and baking powder. Gradually stir flour mixture into butter mixture. Divide dough in half. Roll one half of the dough between two sheets of waxed paper into a 8 x 16-inch (20 x 40 cm) rectangle. Remove top sheet of waxed paper. Spread half the filling over dough to within ¼ inch of edges. Roll up, jelly-roll style, starting from one of the long sides, removing bottom sheet of waxed paper as you roll. Pinch to seal. Cut roll in half crosswise. Wrap rolls in plastic wrap, twisting the ends tightly to seal. Stand the wrapped rolls in tall drinking glasses (this helps them retain their round shape instead of flattening from lying on the refrigerator shelf) and place in the refrigerator. Repeat with remaining dough and filling. Chill about 4 hours or until firm.

Pre-heat oven to 400°F (200°C). Line baking sheets with parchment paper. Remove one roll of dough from the refrigerator. Unwrap and reshape slightly, if necessary. Cut into ¼-inch (0.5 cm) thick slices. Place 2 inches (5 cm) apart on prepared baking sheets.

Bake for 8 to 10 minutes or till edges are lightly browned. Remove from oven and allow to cool for 2 minutes on baking sheets, then remove to wire racks to cool completely.

Store in airtight containers in the refrigerator for up to 2 weeks. Makes 90 cookies. These cookies ship well if wrapped individually to keep them from sticking together.

Chocolate-Cranberry Holiday Bars

Chocolate-Cranberry Holiday Bars

The Wisconsin Milk Marketing Board sent us this festive update to the traditional brownie. The combination of chocolate, cranberries and cream cheese is inspired!

For the bars:

4 ounces (100 g) unsweetened chocolate

½ cup (125 ml) salted butter

¾ cup (175 ml) all-purpose flour

¾ teaspoon (3 ml) salt

2 large eggs

1 cup (250 ml) brown sugar, firmly packed

2 teaspoons (10 ml) vanilla extract

½ cup (125 ml) chopped walnuts

½ cup (125 ml) mini semi-sweet chocolate morsels

For the cranberry cream filling:

½ cup (125 ml) salted butter

4 ounces (100 g) cream cheese, softened

1 teaspoon (5 ml) vanilla extract

1¼ cups (310 ml) powdered sugar

1 cup (250 ml) finely chopped dried cranberries

For the chocolate drizzle:

2 ounces (50 g) semisweet chocolate chips

2 tablespoons (30 ml) whipping cream, or more to achieve desired consistency

Pre-heat oven to 325°F (170°C). Make the bars by melting the chocolate and butter together in a small saucepan or in the microwave, stirring until smooth. Set aside. On a paper plate, whisk together flour and salt; set aside. In a mixing bowl with electric beaters, beat the eggs until fluffy, about 1 minute. Gradually beat in brown sugar. Add the cooled chocolate mixture and vanilla. Stir in flour mixture until blended. Blend in walnuts and chocolate chips. Spread the batter in a buttered 9 x 13-inch (23 x 32 cm) baking pan.

Bake for 20 to 22 minutes or until a toothpick inserted in center comes out clean. Cool in pan on wire rack.

Make the cranberry cream by creaming the butter and cream cheese together in bowl until light and fluffy. Gradually beat in vanilla and powdered sugar; mix in cranberries. Spread mixture over cooled brownies. Refrigerate until set.

Make the drizzle by melting the chocolate chips and whipping cream over low heat or in the microwave. Cool slightly. Dip a fork into the mixture and drizzle over the cranberry layer. Chill until firm. Cut into 2 x 2-inch (5 x 5 cm) bars.

Store in an airtight container in the refrigerator for up to 1 week. Makes 24 bars. These bars should be hand-delivered.

photo courtesy of the Cherry Marketing Insti

Wholesome Granola Bars

Here's the perfect home-made bar for the health nut in your family. We like how the dried cherries add a festive touch. Recipe courtesy of the Cherry Marketing Institute.

1½ cups (375 ml) low fat granola

1 cup (250 ml) quick cooking or old-fashioned oats, uncooked

¾ cup (175 ml) dried tart cherries

½ cup (125 ml) all-purpose flour

⅓ cup (75 ml) slivered almonds, toasted

½ teaspoon (2 ml) ground cinnamon

2 egg whites, slightly beaten

⅓ cup (75 ml) honey

¼ cup (60 ml) firmly packed brown sugar

2 tablespoons (30 ml) vegetable oil

Pre-heat oven to 350°F (180°C). Line bottom and sides of an 8 x 8 x 2-inch (20 x 20 x 5 cm) baking pan with foil. Lightly spray the foil with nonstick spray. Set aside. Combine granola, oats, cherries, flour, almonds and cinnamon in a large mixing bowl. Stir together egg whites, honey, brown sugar and oil. Stir into the cereal mixture, stirring until all is coated. Press mixture evenly into the prepared pan.

Bake 20 to 25 minutes, or until bars are light brown. Place the hot pan on a wire rack and let cool for about 5 minutes. Use foil to remove bars from pan. Let cool completely. Cut into bars.

Store in an airtight container at room temperature for up to 4 weeks. Makes 20 bars. These are great for shipping if individually wrapped to prevent them from sticking.

Scottish Shortbread

This simple recipe is put together quickly in a food processor. The taste is buttery and slightly nutty. Rice flour gives the shortbread its crispy texture.

¾ cup (175 ml) superfine sugar

2½ cups (625 ml) all-purpose flour

¾ cup (175 ml) rice flour

1 teaspoon (5 ml) salt

1½ cup (375 ml) unsalted butter, chilled and chopped into ½-inch (1 cm) cubes

Pre-heat oven to 275°F (140°C). Add sugar, flour, rice flour and salt to food processor. Add cold butter and process until combined. Stop before the mixture forms a ball in the processor. Scrape into a bowl and knead together gently with your hands to form the dough. Divide the dough into thirds.

Roll out a third of the dough into a square about ½ inch (1.5 cm) thick. Cut into 1-inch (2.5 cm) by 3-inch (8 cm) rectangles. Place on ungreased baking sheet and prick with a fork down the length of the rectangle. Repeat with the other two thirds of the dough.

Bake in center of oven for 25 to 30 minutes or until edges just start to turn golden. Remove from oven and let cookies cool directly on the baking sheet.

Store in airtight containers at room temperature for up to 1 month. Makes about 40 cookies. These cookies ship well if packed very carefully and with lots of cushioning.

Cathedral Windows

Cathedral Windows

This was my Grandma's favorite holiday treat. In years when we were too busy to do much baking, we had to have Cathedral Windows at the very least. More candy than cookie, this no-bake snack is simple and fun to make. These will make a colorful addition to your cookie plate, and kids love 'em. —Mimi

½ cup (125 ml) butter, cut into 1-inch (1.5 cm) cubes

2 cups (500 ml) semi-sweet chocolate chips

1 cup (250 ml) chopped walnuts

12 ounces (340 g) colored mini marshmallows (about 9 cups or 2.25 *l*)

2 cups (500 ml) sweetened grated coconut

Heat butter and chocolate chips in the top of a double boiler over low heat, stirring occasionally, until melted and smooth. Set aside to cool slightly. Put marshmallows and nuts in a large bowl; stir in chocolate. Tear five 9-inch (23 cm) sheets of waxed paper and sprinkle each generously with coconut. Divide dough into fifths and place each fifth on a sheet of waxed paper. Roll tightly into 2-inch (5 cm) diameter logs and refrigerate overnight. Before serving, unwrap from waxed paper and cut into ½-inch (1.5 cm) slices.

Store in airtight containers in the refrigerator for up to 1 month. Makes about 60 chocolates. Cathedral Windows ship well in cold weather.

Cheddar Crunch Apple Squares

Cheddar Crunch Apple Squares

This recipe reminds me of something my grandmother used to say every time we ate apple pie: "An apple pie without the cheese is like a kiss without a squeeze." Apples and cheddar make a perfect marriage in these tasty bars. Recipe courtesy of the Wisconsin Milk Marketing Board. —Mimi

1 box (12 ounces or 340 g) vanilla wafers, or 3⅓ cups (825 ml) vanilla wafer crumbs

1½ cup (375 ml) flaked coconut, chopped

½ teaspoon (2 ml) ground cinnamon

1½ cup (375 ml) shredded Wisconsin cheddar cheese

½ cup (125 ml) salted butter, softened

2 cans (21 ounces or 620 ml) apple pie filling

Pre-heat oven to 375°F (190°C). Make crumbs in food processor or with rolling pin and combine with coconut, cinnamon, cheese and butter to form a crumbly mixture. Press one half of this mixture firmly into the bottom of a greased 9 x 12-inch (23 x 30 cm) baking pan. Spread apple pie filling on top of bottom crust. Top with remaining crumb mixture, do not press down.

Bake for about 40 minutes or until golden brown. Cool completely in pan on wire rack in refrigerator and cut into squares about 2 x 2 inches (5 x 5 cm). Serve with cinnamon ice cream or warmed honey.

Store for up to 2 weeks in airtight containers in the refrigerator. Makes 24 squares. These bars should be hand-delivered.

Jackie's Pecan Tartlets

My aunt Jackie Crocker says this recipe, which resembles a miniature pecan pie, is the one must-have cookie her family clamors for every Christmas. I'm not surprised! —Mimi

for the dough:

3 ounces (85 g) cream cheese, softened

½ cup (125 ml) + 1 tablespoon (15 ml) butter, softened

1 cup (250 ml) sifted all-purpose flour

for the filling:

1 large egg

¾ cup (175 ml) brown sugar, firmly packed

1 teaspoon (5 ml) vanilla extract

dash salt

⅔ cup (150 ml) chopped pecans

Combine cream cheese, ½ cup (125 ml) butter & flour. Mix thoroughly and chill, covered, 1 hour.

Pre-heat oven to 325°F (170°C). Divide dough into 24 small balls and press each ball into bottom and up the sides of a mini-muffin cup to form a pastry shell.

Combine egg, brown sugar, vanilla, salt & remaining 1 tablespoon (15 ml) butter; beat until smooth.

Sprinkle ⅓ cup (75 ml) pecans equally into 24 tart shells. Divide egg mixture equally among 24 tarts, pouring on top of pecans. Sprinkle remaining ⅓ cup (75 ml) pecans on top of tarts.

Bake 20-25 minutes or until pastry is golden brown. Run a sharp knife around edges of pastries, then transfer to a rack and cool.

Store in an airtight container in the refrigerator for up to 1 week. Makes 24 tartlets. We recommend hand delivering the tartlets.

Photo courtesy of the California Fig Advisory Board

Old-Fashioned Fig Bars

These traditional fig bars are deliciously moist. Fresh figs, rolled oats, and only a little bit of butter combine to make this cookie a healthier alternative. Recipe courtesy of the California Fig Advisory Board.

California fig filling:

8 ounces (250 g) California figs, Calimyrna or Mission, stems removed, chopped

⅓ cup (75 ml) fruit juice or water

1 teaspoon (5 ml) vanilla

½ to 1 teaspoon (2 to 5 ml) cinnamon, to taste

½ teaspoon (2 ml) nutmeg

For the crust:

1 cup (250 ml) all-purpose flour

1 cup (250 ml) rolled oats

½ cup (125 ml) light brown sugar, firmly packed

1 teaspoon (5 ml) vanilla extract

½ teaspoon (2 ml) salt

⅓ cup (75 ml) butter

Pre-heat oven to 350°F (180°C). For the filling, combine all ingredients in a blender or food processor until puréed. Set aside. For the crust, in a large mixing bowl combine flour, oats, sugar, vanilla and salt. Cut butter into small chunks, then cut into flour mixture with pastry blender or two knives until mixture is blended. Reserve ½ cup (125 ml) of this mixture for the topping. Pat the remaining mixture evenly in the bottom of a 9 x 9 x 2-inch (23 x 23 x 5 cm) square pan. Spread fig filling evenly over crust. Sprinkle with reserved ½ cup (125 ml) topping.

Bake until lightly browned, about 25 to 30 minutes. Allow to cool in pan. Cut into 2-inch (5 cm) squares.

Store in an airtight container in the refrigerator for up to 1 week. Makes 25 squares. Hand delivery is recommended.

Kathy's Nut Roll

Kathy's Nut Roll

This recipe is one of my mother's signature sweets, made first by my grandmother Kay Liebold and my Aunt Mary Walker. The taste of the nutty and sweet filling represents Christmas to me. Everyone still clamors for my mother's recipe, and of course I always give credit to Aunt Mary and my grandmother. —Kristin

for the dough:

¼-ounce (8 g) packet active dry yeast

¼ cup (60 ml) warm water

½ cup (125 ml) granulated sugar

½ cup (125 ml) butter

4 large eggs

4 cups (1ℓ) all-purpose flour

2 teaspoons (10 ml) salt

for the filling:

4 cups (1ℓ) chopped pecans or walnuts

½ cup (125 ml) brown sugar, firmly packed

½ cup (125 ml) granulated sugar

½ cup (125 ml) butter, melted

2 large eggs, beaten

¼ cup (60 ml) butter, melted

Dissolve yeast in ¼ cup (60 ml) warm water. Beat the sugar and butter until light and fluffy. Stir in eggs, one at a time, mixing until fully combined before each addition. Add yeast to butter mixture, mix well. Sift together 4 cups (1𝘭) all-purpose flour and 2 teaspoons (10 ml) salt. Gradually stir into butter mixture. Place in a greased bowl, cover and refrigerate overnight.

Stir together nuts, granulated sugar, brown sugar, melted butter and eggs. Mix well.

Divide dough in half and return one half to the refrigerator. Roll dough out to 10 x 14 inches (25 x 35 cm). Spread half of the filling over the dough and roll up, starting from the short side of the rectangle. Repeat with the rest of the dough and filling. Seal edges, cover with towel and place in warm spot until dough rises, or for 1 hour.

Pre-heat oven to 350°F (180°C). Place rolls on a greased baking sheet and bake for 30 minutes. Remove rolls from the oven and brush tops with melted butter. Return to the oven and continue baking 15 minutes. Let cool on baking sheet and slice.

Store in an airtight container in the refrigerator for up to 1 week. Makes 2 nut rolls, approximately 15 slices in each. We recommend you hand-deliver this pastry, preferably on the day it is baked. Freezes well.

Eggnog Sparkle Cookies

Eggnog Sparkle Cookies

This is a simple and tasty cookie that will be sure to brighten up your cookie tray. Recipe courtesy of the Wisconsin Milk Marketing Board.

For the cookie:

1 cup (500 ml) salted butter, softened

1 cup (250 ml) granulated sugar

2 egg yolks

½ cup (125 ml) eggnog

2½ cups (625 ml) all-purpose flour

2 teaspoons (10 ml) baking powder

1 teaspoon (5 ml) ground nutmeg

For the topping:

⅓ cup (75 ml) red decorating sugar

1 teaspoon (5 ml) ground cinnamon

In a large mixing bowl, beat butter and sugar until fluffy. Beat in egg yolks until combined. Add eggnog. Whisk together flour, baking powder and nutmeg; stir into butter mixture until thoroughly combined. Wrap dough in plastic wrap and refrigerate 2 hours or until firm.

Pre-heat oven to 400°F (205°C). Lightly butter two baking sheets. Combine topping ingredients on a paper plate. Roll dough into 1-inch (2.5 cm) diameter balls; roll in topping mixture.

Place 2 inches (5 cm) apart on prepared baking sheets. Bake 8 to 10 minutes or until set. Allow to cool 1 minute on the baking sheet and then remove to wire racks to cool thoroughly.

Store in an airtight container at room temperature for up to 4 weeks. Makes about 60 cookies. These cookies are great shippers.

Variation: For variety, other colored sugars can be used for the topping in place of the red sugar and cinnamon.

Kathy's Lemon Bars

On a chilly Christmas Eve, lemon restores a bit of sunshine, especially in these tangy, tart bars. These bars are perfect with coffee, tea, cappuccino or cocoa.
— Kristin

¾ cup (175 ml) butter

1½ cup (375 ml) all-purpose flour

⅓ cup (75 ml) powdered sugar

4 large eggs

2 cups (500 ml) granulated sugar

¼ cup (60 ml) all-purpose flour

1 teaspoon (5 ml) baking powder

dash salt

6 tablespoons (90 ml) lemon juice

additional powdered sugar

Pre-heat oven to 350°F (180°C), or 325°F (170°C) if you are using a glass baking pan. Stir together butter, 1½ (375 ml) cup flour, and ⅓ cup (75 ml) powdered sugar, until well blended. Pat into the bottom of a 9 x 13-inch (23 x 32 cm) baking pan. Bake 18 minutes or until just barely golden.

Beat together the eggs, sugar, ¼ cup (60 ml) flour, baking powder, salt, and lemon juice. Pour on top of crust and spread evenly. Return to oven and bake up to an additional 25 minutes or until set, watching so that cookies don't burn. Remove from oven and sprinkle with additional powdered sugar. Cut into bars.

Store in the refrigerator in airtight containers for up to 1 week. Makes 36 bars. These bars are best for hand delivery.

Yeast Crisps

Yeast Crisps

This unusual cookie is another of my Grandma's delicious recipes. These thin, delicate cookies are incredibly light and flaky, with a bit of a yeasty flavor reminiscent of a glazed doughnut. —Mimi

¼-ounce (8 g) packet active dry yeast

⅓ cup (75 ml) warm water

1 cup (250 ml) butter, softened

⅛ teaspoon (0.5 ml) salt

2 cups (500 ml) all-purpose flour

1 cup (250 ml) granulated sugar

flour and sugar for rolling

Put warm water in a small bowl and stir the yeast into the water. Set aside. Mix together margarine, salt and flour; stir in yeast mixture and blend well. Chill for 1 hour.

Put the sugar in a small bowl. Form 1-inch (2.5 cm) diameter balls of dough and roll them in the sugar. Place the balls in a shallow pan and chill for 30 minutes.

Pre-heat oven to 350°F (180°C). Line baking sheets with parchment paper. The parchment paper is very important because these thin, delicate cookies are almost impossible to remove from the baking sheet in one piece without it. Use the parchment even if you have a non-stick baking sheet; otherwise, the dark surface of the non-stick coating will cause your cookies to brown too fast. If you don't have parchment handy, use brown paper.

Dust a work surface and rolling pin with a mixture of flour and sugar for rolling out the cookies. Working with one cookie at a time, place a ball on the work surface and press it flat with the ball of your hand. Turn it over and press again. This coats the ball with some flour and sugar to keep it from sticking. Roll out the dough very thinly, about 1/16 inch (2 mm) or less, or until the dough makes a rectangle about 3 x 4 inches (8 x 10 cm), then cut in half crosswise. Pick up the very thin dough with a sharp wide knife, such as a chef's knife, using the wide blade like a spatula (a regular spatula is generally too thick to slide under the thin and delicate dough), and place the cookie on your prepared baking sheet.

Let rest for at least 30 seconds then bake for 6 to 8 minutes or until crisps are golden brown. Remove from oven and let cool 1 minute. Remove to a wire rack to cool completely.

Store in an airtight container at room temperature. These cookies are best made up to 1 day before serving because they tend to lose their crispness quickly in humid climates. However, you can make them up to 2 weeks ahead of time and re-crisp them in a 300°F (160°C) oven for 5 minutes before serving. Makes about 100 crisps. The crisps are best if hand-delivered.

Variation: Use cinnamon sugar or vanilla sugar instead of plain sugar.

photo courtesy of the Cranberry Marketing Committee

Apple Cranberry Tea Ring

Apple Cranberry Tea Ring

This is perfect to bring to a holiday brunch. Your hostess will be thrilled to place it on her banquet table! It looks very impressive and tastes even better. Recipe courtesy of the Cranberry Marketing Committee.

for the bread:

3 cups (750 ml) all-purpose flour

3 tablespoons (45 ml) granulated sugar

¼-ounce (8 g) packet Red Star® Active Dry Yeast

1 tablespoon (15 ml) grated orange zest

1 teaspoon (5 ml) salt

½ cup (125 ml) milk

¼ cup (60 ml) water

2 tablespoons (30 ml) butter

1 large egg

for the egg wash:

1 tablespoon (15 ml) water

1 egg white

for the filling:

½ cup (125 ml) granulated sugar

2 teaspoons (10 ml) ground cinnamon

1 cup (250 ml) peeled, thinly sliced apples

1 cup (250 ml) dried cranberries

¾ cup (175 ml) nuts, toasted and chopped

for the glaze:

½ cup (125 ml) powdered sugar

1 to 2 tablespoons (15 to 30 ml) orange juice

1 teaspoon (5 ml) grated orange zest

To make the bread, oil the inside of a medium mixing bowl; set aside. In a separate bowl, blend 1 cup (250 ml) flour with sugar, yeast, orange zest and salt; set aside. In a small saucepan over low heat, heat milk, water and butter until warm (120°F or 49°C); pour into a large bowl. Add flour mixture. With an electric mixer, blend on low for 30 seconds; add egg. Beat on medium for 3 minutes. Stir in remaining flour. Knead on floured surface for 5 to 8 minutes until dough is smooth and elastic. Place dough in the oiled bowl, turning the dough over once so that oil coats both sides. Cover with a towel and let rise in a warm place until double in size, about 1 hour.

Meanwhile, grease one baking sheet; set aside.

Turn out the dough onto a lightly floured surface and punch it down to remove air. Roll into a 15 x 12-inch (38 x 30 cm) rectangle.

For the egg wash, blend the egg white and water; brush over dough. Refrigerate remaining egg wash.

For the filling, combine sugar and cinnamon; sprinkle over dough. Top with apples, cranberries and nuts, distributing evenly over dough to within 1 inch (2.5 cm) of edges. Starting with long side of dough, roll into a log; pinch to seal the long edge. Form log into a ring, overlap and seal the ends. Place seam side down on prepared baking sheet. Using scissors, cut ring from outside through all dough layers to within 1 inch (2.5 cm) of center. Make 12 cuts, 2 inches (5 cm) apart. Twist each cut section ¾ turn so cut side faces downward forming a pinwheel. Cover with a damp cloth and let rise in a warm place until indentation remains after touching side, about 30 minutes.

Meanwhile, pre-heat oven to 375°F (190°C).

Brush dough with remaining egg wash. Bake for 30 to 40 minutes or until golden brown; cool.

For the glaze, blend powdered sugar, orange juice and orange zest. Drizzle over cooled tea ring.

Cover loosely with plastic wrap and store in the refrigerator. This is best eaten within a day or two of being made. Serves 12. Hand delivery is recommended.

photo courtesy of the American Dairy Association

Clockwise from top: Chocolate Lace Cookies, Cream Cheese Spritz, and Ricotta Cheese Cookies

Chocolate Lace Cookies

Lace cookies are an elegant accompaniment to a dish of ice cream, pudding or custard. They are also wonderful all by themselves. Here we've dressed up the traditional lace cookie with a little chocolate.

⅔ cup (150 ml) butter

2 cups (500 ml) quick-cooking rolled oats

1 cup (250 ml) granulated sugar

⅔ cup (150 ml) all-purpose flour

¼ cup (60 ml) corn syrup

¼ cup (60 ml) milk

1 teaspoon (5 ml) vanilla extract

¼ teaspoon (1 ml) salt

2 cups (500 ml) semi-sweet chocolate morsels

Pre-heat oven to 375°F (190°C). Line 2 baking sheets with aluminum foil. Melt butter in a medium saucepan over low heat. Remove from heat. Stir in oats, sugar, flour, corn syrup, milk, vanilla extract and salt; mix well. Drop by teaspoonfuls, about 4 inches (10 cm) apart, onto prepared baking sheets. Spread into 2-inch (5 cm) diameter circles.

Bake 5-7 minutes, or until the edges are golden brown. Remove from oven and allow to cool several minutes on baking sheet. Peel foil away from cookies. If foil doesn't come off easily, return to oven for a couple more minutes.

In the top of a double boiler over hot (not boiling) water, melt chocolate morsels; stir until smooth. Spread chocolate on smooth side of half of the cookies. Top with remaining cookies while chocolate is still warm. Allow chocolate to cool and harden before serving.

Store between sheets of waxed paper in an airtight container at room temperature for up to 5 days. Makes 40 cookies. These cookies are best for hand delivery.

Variation: While still warm, roll cookies around the handle of a wooden spoon to make a cigar shape. When cool, dip each end in melted chocolate.

Ricotta Cheese Cookies

This is one of the top-rated cookies at Christmas-Cookies.com. It's quick and easy to make, tastes delicious, and looks very pretty! In short, the perfect Christmas cookie recipe for small children and busy moms. It makes a huge quantity of cookies, but the recipe can be halved.

for the cookies:

1 cup (250 ml) butter, softened

2 cups (500 ml) granulated sugar

1 (15-ounce or 500 g) container of ricotta cheese

1 tablespoon (15 ml) vanilla extract

1 teaspoon (5 ml) salt

1 teaspoon (5 ml) baking soda

4 cups (1 *l*) all-purpose flour

for the glaze:

1 cup (250 ml) powdered sugar

1 tablespoon (15 ml) milk

sprinkles, jimmies, or colored sugar

Pre-heat oven to 350°F (180°C). In a large mixing bowl, beat together the butter and sugar until light and fluffy. Set aside. In a medium bowl, stir together the salt, baking soda, and flour. Gradually stir the flour mixture into the ricotta cheese mixture, mixing until the dough sticks together into a big ball. It will be sticky. Drop by teaspoonfuls on an ungreased cookie sheet.

Bake 10 minutes or until the bottoms turn golden brown. Let cool for 1 minute and then transfer to wire racks to cool completely.

In a small saucepan slowly stir milk into the powdered sugar until it creates a glaze thin enough to be spread over the cookies. You may need more or less milk depending on the heat and humidity in your kitchen. Stir mixture over low heat, then spread over cooled cookies. Quickly top with sprinkles, jimmies, or colored sugar.

Store in an airtight container in the refrigerator for up to 2 weeks. Makes 100 cookies. Since they are frosted, these cookies are best for hand delivery. Unfrosted, they are great for shipping.

Cream Cheese Spritz

The cream cheese in this recipe enhances the flavor of the traditional Spritz butter cookie and gives it a softer texture.

½ cup (125 ml) butter, slightly softened

1½ ounces (42.5 g) cream cheese, slightly softened

¼ cup (60 ml) granulated sugar

½ teaspoon (2 ml) vanilla extract

1 cup (250 ml) sifted all-purpose flour

food color (optional)

colored sugar, sprinkles, and dragées (optional)

Pre-heat oven to 375°F (190°C). Beat butter and cream cheese until light and fluffy. Beat in the sugar and vanilla. Slowly add the sifted flour, mix well. If desired, tint dough with a few drops of food color. Fill a cookie press with the dough and form cookies on an ungreased baking sheet. If desired, decorate with colored sugar, sprinkles, or dragées.

Bake 8 to 10 minutes. Remove from oven and allow to cool 1 minute on baking sheet. Remove to a wire rack to cool completely.

Store in an airtight container at room temperature for up to 1 month. Makes 24 cookies. These little cookies are excellent shippers.

photo courtesy of the California Pistachio Commission

Pistachio Cookie Tree

Pistachio Cookie Tree

Here is a fun project for people who enjoy baking and crafts. It would make a fabulous gift for your hostess to place as a centerpiece on her dessert table. Recipe courtesy of the California Pistachio Commission.

3 cups (750 ml) butter or margarine, at room temperature

2¼ cups (560 ml) granulated sugar

3 egg yolks

4 teaspoons (20 ml) pistachio or almond extract

7 cups (1.75 *l*) all-purpose flour

4 cups (1 *l*) natural California pistachios, finely chopped, divided

2 (4.25-ounce or 120 g) tubes white decorating icing

Inshell pistachios, for tree top decoration

¼-inch (0.5 cm) diameter wooden dowel, 10 inches (25 cm) long

½-inch (1.5 cm) thick plywood, cut into 8-inch (20 cm) diameter circle

carpenter's glue

cardboard, cut into a 3-inch (8 cm) star

Pre-heat oven to 350°F (180°C). Line 2 baking sheets with parchment paper. In a large bowl, beat butter until creamy. Beat in sugar, egg yolk and extract. Gradually stir in flour and 3 cups chopped pistachios. Divide dough into 4 equal portions. Roll out on floured board to ¼-inch (0.5 cm) thickness. Cut into oval "cloud" shapes of three different sizes, making equal numbers of each size.* Gently drill ¼-inch (0.5 cm) hole slightly off-center in each, using a chopstick or dowel. Place on prepared baking sheets. Bake for 10 minutes, then cover loosely with foil to prevent excessive browning. Continue baking for 12 to 14 minutes or until centers are crisp. Remove from oven and allow to cool on baking sheets until sturdy enough to move. Remove to wire racks to cool completely.

To assemble tree, drill a ¼-inch (0.5 cm) diameter hole in the center of the plywood circle. Put a couple of drops of glue in the hole, then insert the dowel into the hole. Glue inshell pistachios onto cardboard star. Allow glue to dry. Pipe icing onto outer edge of each cookie and sprinkle with remaining chopped pistachios while icing is still wet. When dry, stack cookies on dowel, placing the large "clouds" on the bottom, then the medium "clouds," and finally the small "clouds" on top, to make a Christmas tree shape. Top tree with cardboard star decorated with inshell pistachios.

This tree will keep at room temperature for about 1 week, or much longer if you don't intend to eat it. We recommend hand-delivering the cookie tree.

* *Suggested measurements:* 6½ inches (16.5 cm), 5½ inches (14 cm), and 4½ inches (10 cm) across.

Judy's Pecan Balls

Judy's Pecan Balls

This has become a classic in my family and my grandma attributed it to my Aunt Judy. It is essential to use cake flour in this recipe, because that's what gives the cookies that crumbly, melt-in-your-mouth texture. —Mimi

¾ cup (175 ml) ground pecans

1 cup (250 ml) butter, softened

½ cup (125 ml) powdered sugar

1 teaspoon (5 ml) vanilla extract

2¼ cups (560 ml) cake flour

¼ teaspoon (1 ml) salt

powdered sugar

Stir together pecans, butter, ½ cup (125 ml) powdered sugar and vanilla, mix well. Sift together flour and salt, and then gradually stir into nut mixture. Wrap in plastic wrap and chill in the refrigerator for 2 hours. Pre-heat oven to 350°F (180°C). Roll dough into 1-inch (2.5 cm) balls, then roll each ball 3 times in the extra powdered sugar. Place 2 inches (5 cm) apart on an ungreased baking sheet.

Bake for 8 to 10 minutes or until set but not brown. Allow to cool for 2 minutes on baking sheet and remove to wire rack to cool completely. If desired, dust with powdered sugar before serving.

Store in an airtight container in the refrigerator for up to 1 month. Makes 48 cookies. These cookies can be shipped if packaged carefully.

Apricot Foldovers

Apricot Foldovers

This is another of my Grandma's unusual but delicious recipes. This cookie with the light and flaky pastry provides the perfect balance of savory and sweet. For the best flavor make sure to use sharp cheddar cheese. —Mimi

½ cup (125 ml) butter, softened

1 cup (250 ml) sharp cheddar cheese, finely grated

1⅓ cup (325 ml) sifted all-purpose flour

2 tablespoons (30 ml) water

½ cup (125 ml) apricot preserves

½ cup (125 ml) granulated sugar

Beat the butter and cheese until light and fluffy, then blend in the flour and water until just combined. Chill the dough for 4 to 5 hours.

Pre-heat the oven to 375°F (190°C). In a medium saucepan over medium heat, heat the preserves and sugar until the mixture boils and is smooth. Set aside to cool. Divide the dough in half. Roll each half into a 10-inch (25 cm) square, cut into 2½-inch (6.5 cm) squares. Put 1 teaspoon (5 ml) of the preserves in the center of each square, fold over diagonally and seal the edges with the tines of a fork.

Bake on an ungreased baking sheet for 8 to 10 minutes or until edges are lightly browned. Allow to cool for 1 minute then transfer to wire racks to cool completely.

Store in airtight containers in the refrigerator for up to 1 week. Makes about 30 cookies. These cookies should be hand-delivered.

Cherry Biscotti

Cherry Biscotti

The red cherries in these biscotti give them a cheery and festive appearance. For an even more Christmasy look, substitute chopped green pistachios for the walnuts. Recipe courtesy of the Cherry Marketing Institute.

¾ cup (175 ml) granulated sugar

2 large eggs

¼ cup (60 ml) vegetable oil

1 tablespoon (15 ml) orange juice

2 teaspoons (10 ml) grated orange zest

1½ teaspoons (7 ml) vanilla extract

2 cups (500 ml) all-purpose flour

½ cup (125 ml) finely chopped walnuts

1 teaspoon (5 ml) baking powder

¼ teaspoon (1 ml) salt

1 cup (250 ml) chopped dried tart cherries

1 egg white

1 tablespoon (15 ml) water

additional granulated sugar

Pre-heat oven to 350°F (180°C). Grease one baking sheet. Combine ¾ cup (175 ml) sugar and eggs in a large mixing bowl. Beat with an electric mixer at medium speed, scraping bowl often, 2 to 3 minutes, or until thick and pale yellow in color. Add oil, orange juice, orange peel and vanilla; beat 1 to 2 minutes, or until well mixed. Combine flour, walnuts, baking powder and salt; gradually add to egg mixture. Mix on low speed 1 to 2 minutes, or until well mixed. Stir in cherries by hand.

Turn dough onto lightly floured surface (dough will be soft and sticky). Lightly sprinkle with additional flour; knead flour into dough. With floured hands, shape into 2 (8 x 2-inch or 20 x 5 cm) logs. Place 3 to 4 inches (7 to 10 cm) apart on prepared baking sheet; flatten tops slightly. Combine egg white and water; brush on logs. Sprinkle with additional granulated sugar.

Bake 25 to 30 minutes, or until light brown and firm to the touch. Let cool on baking sheet 15 minutes.

Reduce oven temperature to 300°F (150°C). Cut logs diagonally into ½-inch (1.5 cm) slices with a serrated knife; arrange slices, cut side down, on baking sheet. Bake 8 to 10 minutes; turn slices. Bake another 8 to 10 minutes, or until golden brown. Remove to wire rack; let cool completely.

Store in an airtight container at room temperature for up to 1 month. Makes 30 biscotti. These are great for shipping.

Cranberry Spice Bread

Cranberry Spice Bread

Quick breads are a favorite to give and receive at Christmastime. Lower in fat and sugar than most holiday desserts, they're a delicious alternative for those who are watching their weight over the holidays but don't want to miss out on all the goodies. Here's our favorite festive loaf.

2 cups (500 ml) flour

¾ cup (175 ml) brown sugar, firmly packed

2 teaspoons (10 ml) baking powder

½ teaspoon (2 ml) salt

1 teaspoon (5 ml) ground cinnamon

½ teaspoon (2 ml) ground nutmeg

¼ teaspoon (1 ml) ground cloves

¾ cup (175 ml) whole milk

6 tablespoons (90 ml) melted butter or canola oil

1 egg, lightly beaten

1 teaspoon (5 ml) hazelnut or almond extract

1 tablespoon (15 ml) grated orange zest

1 cup (250 ml) fresh or frozen cranberries, halved

1 cup (250 ml) sliced hazelnuts or almonds

Pre-heat oven to 325°F (170°C). Grease a 9 x 5-inch (23 x 13 cm) loaf pan. In a large bowl stir together the flour, sugar, baking powder, salt and spices.

In another bowl, combine the milk, melted butter or oil, egg, orange zest and almond extract. Stir the flour mixture into the milk mixture. Fold in the cranberries and almonds.

Pour batter into prepared loaf pan and spread evenly. Bang the pan twice on the counter to remove any air pockets. Bake for 1 hour and 10 minutes, or until the top is golden and a toothpick inserted in the center comes out clean. Cool the bread in the pan for 10 minutes and then turn onto a rack to cool completely.

Wrap in plastic wrap and store in the refrigerator for up to 1 week. Makes one loaf. Hand delivery is recommended.

Whipped Shortbread

Whipped Shortbread

These light and airy cookies just melt in your mouth. The dough is very easy to work with, and you can use your cookie press to create any shape you want.

2 cups (500 ml) butter, softened

1 cup (250 ml) powdered sugar

1 teaspoon (5 ml) vanilla

pinch salt

½ cup (125 ml) cornstarch

3 cups (750 ml) all-purpose flour

candied cherries (optional)

Pre-heat oven to 350°F (180°C). Beat together butter, powdered sugar, vanilla and salt until creamy. Gradually stir in cornstarch and flour. Whip with an electric mixer until light and fluffy. Place into a pastry bag fitted with a large star tip and press out 2-inch (5 cm) diameter circles onto an ungreased baking sheet. If desired, decorate with candied cherries.

Bake 12-15 minutes. Let cool for 2 minutes on baking sheet, then remove to wire rack to cool completely.

Store in an airtight container at room temperature for up to 1 month. Makes about 40 cookies. These cookies are very delicate, so we recommend you hand-deliver them.

Springerle

These traditional German cookies have a subtle anise flavor similar to licorice and are dry and hard, making them perfect for dunking in coffee or tea. They are traditionally made with a Springerle mold or roller, sold at specialty cooking stores, or you can cut them into shapes with a knife or cookie cutters.

2 tablespoons (30 ml) anise seed, crushed

4 large eggs

2 cups (500 ml) sugar

½ teaspoon (2 ml) anise extract or ¼ teaspoon (1 ml) anise oil

zest of 1 lemon, finely grated

4½ cups (1.25 ℓ) cake flour, sifted

Line 2 baking sheets with parchment paper; evenly scatter the crushed anise seeds over the parchment. Beat eggs until very light and fluffy. Gradually add sugar, beat for at least 15 minutes, until mixture is very light and creamy. Do not underbeat. Fold in anise extract or oil, lemon zest, and flour. Dough will be sticky. On a floured board, with a well-floured rolling pin, roll dough to ⅜ inch (1 cm) thick. Thoroughly flour a Springerle mold or rolling pin. Press mold firmly to dough. Cut cookies apart and place on prepared baking sheets. Let dry overnight or for several hours at room temperature (this helps them retain the impressions from the mold during baking).

Pre-heat oven to 375°F (190°C). Place cookies in oven and immediately reduce the temperature to 300°F (150°C). Bake for 15 minutes. Cookies should not brown. Allow to cool for 1 minute on baking sheet and then remove to a wire rack to cool completely.

Store cookies for up to 3 months in an airtight container at room temperature. Many people think that Springerle should be allowed to age and mellow for 2 to 3 weeks before being eaten. Makes about 60 cookies. These cookies are perfect for shipping.

Easy Triple Chocolate Caramel Brownies

These incredibly chewy, gooey, chocolaty bars are adapted from the classic "Knock You Naked Brownies" recipe from the Salt Creek Restaurant in Breckenridge, Colorado. We like how using a mix simplifies the process but they taste absolutely homemade!

1 (18.5-ounce or 525 g) package German chocolate cake mix

1 cup (250 ml) chopped pecans

⅓ cup (75 ml) + ½ cup (125 ml) evaporated milk, divided

½ cup (125 ml) melted butter

60 chocolate-flavored caramel candies, unwrapped (one 14-ounce or 850 g package)

1 cup (250 ml) semi-sweet chocolate chips

Pre-heat oven to 350°F (180°C). Grease a 9 x 13-inch (23 x 32 cm) glass baking pan. In a large mixing bowl, combine dry cake mix, pecans, ⅓ cup (75 ml) evaporated milk and melted butter. Press half of the batter into the bottom of the pan. Bake for 8 minutes.

Meanwhile, in the microwave or the top of a double boiler melt the caramels with the remaining ½ cup (125 ml) evaporated milk; stir. When the caramel mixture is well blended, pour it on top of the baked layer and spread it out to the edges and corners of the pan. Scatter the chocolate chips evenly on top of the warm caramel. Chill for about an hour or until the caramel is firm.

Crumble the remaining batter evenly on top of the caramel layer. Return to oven and bake 18 minutes. Cool completely. Cut into 2-inch (5 cm) squares.

Store in airtight containers in the refrigerator for up to 2 weeks. Makes 30 bars. These brownies ship well if individually wrapped to keep the caramel from making them stick together.

Clockwise from top: Butterball Santas, Fancy Chocolate Tarts, Festive Eggnog Peppermint Twists

Fancy Chocolate Tarts

We love this recipe because it looks and tastes like you worked very hard making hand-made chocolates, but actually you can whip these up in minutes. Perfect for a busy guest to offer to the hostess at a holiday dinner. Recipe courtesy of the Wisconsin Milk Marketing Board.

1 cup (250 ml) milk chocolate chips

8 ounces (250 g) Wisconsin Mascarpone or cream cheese, room temperature

24 small chocolate shell cups or small frozen filo dough cups, thawed

Decorative sprinkles or maraschino cherries for garnish

In the top of a double boiler over low heat, melt chocolate chips; cool slightly. In a mixing bowl, beat Mascarpone or cream cheese until smooth. Stir in melted chocolate; beat with electric mixer at medium speed for two minutes. Transfer mixture to a pastry bag fitted with a large star tip. Pipe mixture into chocolate or filo cups; top with garnish; chill until firm. Makes 24. Hand delivery is recommended.

Note: If you can't find pre-made chocolate shell cups, you can make your own by melting 1½ cups semi-sweet chocolate chips and spreading a layer of melted chocolate on the inside of 24 miniature foil candy cups. Chill until chocolate is firm, then carefully peel foil away from cups.

Butterball Santas

These adorable Santas will bring a smile to anyone's face. Whether you make them yourself or receive them as a gift, they are sure to bring out the kid in you. Recipe courtesy of the Wisconsin Milk Marketing Board.

1 cup (250 ml) unsalted butter, at room temperature

½ cup (125 ml) granulated sugar

1 tablespoon (15 ml) milk

1 teaspoon (5 ml) vanilla extract

2¼ cups (560 ml) all-purpose flour

½ teaspoon (2 ml) red paste or gel food coloring*

60 miniature chocolate chips

1 (4.25-ounce or 120 g) tube purchased white decorator frosting

*You may use traditional red liquid food coloring, but it will take a larger amount to achieve the same vibrant color.

Pre-heat oven to 325°F (170°C). Using a mixer, beat butter until fluffy. Add sugar; beat until well combined. Beat in milk and vanilla extract. Beat in flour. If you are not using a heavy duty mixer, it will be necessary to beat in the last of the flour by hand. Remove one cup of dough and set aside. Beat food coloring into remaining dough to make a bright red tone.

Form the plain and red doughs into 12 equally sized balls each. With red dough, separate each ball into one 1-inch (2.5 cm) ball and five ½-inch

(1.25 cm) balls. With plain dough, separate each of the balls into one ¾-inch (2 cm) ball and four ¼-inch (0.75 cm) balls.

Shape the Santas (see photo): Slightly flatten the 1-inch (2.5 cm) red ball on an ungreased cookie sheet. This is Santa's "body." Place plain ¾-inch (2 cm) ball on top of red ball for head; flatten slightly. Attach the four red ½-inch (1.25 cm) balls for arms and legs. Attach the last red ball as a cap on top of Santa's head. Reshape cap slightly to form a triangle. Attach the four ¼-inch (0.75 cm) plain balls for Santa's hands and feet. Lightly press the balls against each other so they hold together. Add miniature chocolate chips to face for eyes and nose, and to body for buttons.

Bake 12 to 15 minutes or until lightly browned. Remove from oven and allow to cool for two minutes on baking sheet. Remove to wire racks to cool completely.

Using star tip, squeeze the decorator frosting to form a mustache and beard on Santa's face. Then, form a ball at the tip of his cap and rim at the bottom of his hat, and outline his coat (see photo).

Store in an airtight container at room temperature for up to 3 weeks. Makes 12 Santas. Hand delivery is recommended, but they will ship well if you omit the frosting.

Festive Eggnog Peppermint Twists

These cookies are indeed festive with their bright holiday colors and eggnog-peppermint flavor. Recipe courtesy of the Wisconsin Milk Marketing Board.

¾ cup (175 ml) butter, at room temperature

¾ cup (175 ml) granulated sugar

¼ teaspoon (1 ml) baking powder

¼ teaspoon (1 ml) salt

1 large egg

⅓ cup (75 ml) prepared dairy eggnog

1 teaspoon (5 ml) pure vanilla extract

½ teaspoon (2 ml) peppermint extract

2½ to 3 cups (625 to 750 ml) all-purpose flour

¼ teaspoon (1 ml) red paste or gel food coloring*

¼ teaspoon (1 ml) green paste or gel food coloring*

1 (4.25-ounce or 120 g) tube prepared white decorator frosting

*You may use traditional liquid food coloring, but it will require a larger quantity to achieve the same vibrant colors.

Pre-heat oven to 375°F (190°C). Using an electric mixer, beat butter on high for 30 seconds. Add sugar, baking powder and salt. Beat until well blended. Beat in egg, eggnog, vanilla and peppermint extract. Beat in enough flour to make a stiff dough. You may have to finish beating by hand if you are not using a heavy duty mixer.

Divide dough in half. Color half with red coloring and half with green by mixing in coloring pastes. Cover portions and refrigerate until easy to handle, at least 30 minutes.

Lightly flour a working surface and shape each dough portion into a 12-inch (30 cm) log. Cut each log into 24 portions, each ½-inch (1.5 cm) long. With your palms, roll each portion into a 6-inch (15 cm) long rope. Place a red and green rope side-by-side. Twist one rope over the other, gently pressing the ends together, into either a wreath shape or a candy cane shape. Repeat with remaining red and green ropes. Place on ungreased cookie sheets about two inches apart.

Bake for 8 to 10 minutes. Cool on cookie sheets for one minute. Carefully transfer to wire racks to cool completely. Using a decorator tip, pipe the tube frosting to form bows on the wreaths and canes.

Store in airtight containers at room temperature for up to 3 weeks if undecorated, 5 days if decorated. If decorated with frosting, store them in layers with tissue paper separating each layer. Makes 24 cookies. These cookies ship well if packed carefully, but we recommend you ship them unfrosted.

photo courtesy of the California Pistachio Commission

Pistachio Christmas Ribbon Bars

These bars are one of the top-rated cookies at Christmas-Cookies.com. They are not only easy and delicious, they also look very festive with red jam and the green pistachios. Recipe courtesy of the California Pistachio Commission.

1 cup (250 ml) butter or margarine

1 cup (250 ml) granulated sugar

1 large egg

2 cups (500 ml) all-purpose flour

⅛ teaspoon (0.5 ml) salt

½ to ⅔ cup (125 ml to 200 ml) raspberry or strawberry jam, apricot preserves or marmalade

⅔ cup (200 ml) chopped natural California pistachios

Pre-heat oven to 325°F (170°C). Combine butter, sugar and egg; beat until thoroughly blended. Stir in flour and salt. Spread one half of dough into 9-inch (23 cm) square* pan. Bake for 10 minutes; remove from oven. Spread jam to within ½ inch (1.5 cm) of edge. Add pistachios to remaining dough. Drop by spoonfuls over jam to cover. Bake 35 minutes until top is golden brown; cool. Cut into bars.

Makes 24 to 32 cookies. Store in an airtight container in the refrigerator for up to 2 weeks. These bars are best for hand delivery.

Serving Tip: For a special dessert, serve warm 3-inch (8 cm) square bars topped with whipped cream and additional chopped pistachios.

 * A 7½ x 11½ x 1¾-inch (19 x 29 x 4.5-cm) pan can be substituted.

Grandma's Fattigmann

Grandma's Fattigmann

My mother and I can't remember a Christmas that my grandma didn't make these. Grandma said these "Poor Man's Cakes" are Norwegian in origin but we never found out where she got the recipe—she wasn't Norwegian!   —Mimi

2 eggs, lightly beaten

1 tablespoon (15 ml) sugar

3 tablespoons (45 ml) heavy cream

1 teaspoon (5 ml) crushed cardamom

½ teaspoon (2 ml) salt

1¾ cups (425 ml) all-purpose flour

vegetable oil for frying

powdered sugar

Beat together eggs, sugar, and cream. Blend in cardamom or brandy and salt. Gradually stir in flour and mix well to make a smooth dough. Roll out to ¹⁄₁₆ inch (2 ml) thickness. With a knife or a fluted pastry wheel, cut into 2½ x 4-inch (4 x 6.5 cm) rectangles. Make a slit lengthwise in the center and slip one end through slit to make a bow. In a heavy saucepan or a deep fryer, heat oil to 350°F (180°C). Drop cookies into oil, a few at a time, frying until delicately browned, about 1½ minutes. Drain on paper towels. Dust with powdered sugar.

These are best eaten the day they are made, but you can store them in an airtight container at room temperature for about 2 weeks and re-crisp them by putting them in a 300°F (150°C) oven for about 5 minutes. Makes about 60 cookies. Fattigmann should be hand-delivered.

photo courtesy of the California Pistachio Commission

Pistachio Cream Cheese Butter Cookies

With this recipe you get 3 cookies for the price of one! You can triple the recipe and make one batch of each cookie, or make the regular recipe and divide it in thirds so you can try a small batch of each one. Recipe courtesy of the California Pistachio Commission.

1 cup (250 ml) butter or margarine, softened

6 ounces (170 g) cream cheese

⅔ cup (150 ml) granulated sugar

1 egg yolk

2½ cups (625 ml) all-purpose flour

1 tablespoon (15 ml) grated lemon zest

1 tablespoon (15 ml) lemon juice

½ cup (125 ml) shelled natural California pistachios, finely chopped

additional chopped pistachios (for Jamprints and Swedish Bars)

sifted powdered sugar (for Jamprints)

jam or lemon curd (for Jamprints and Swedish Bars)

additional granulated sugar (for Lemon Twists)

Pre-heat oven to 350°F (180°C). Beat together butter, cream cheese and sugar until light and fluffy. Beat in egg yolk, stir in flour, lemon zest, juice and pistachios until well mixed. If dough gets too stiff for the mixer, work in the last of the flour by kneading on a board. Form desired shapes and bake as directed (see below).

For Jamprints: Shape scant tablespoon (15 ml) portions of dough into balls. Roll half the balls in additional finely chopped pistachios; leave other half plain. Place 2 inches (5 cm) apart on ungreased baking sheets. Bake about 14 minutes or until set. Allow to cool for about 2 minutes. Create an indent in the warm cookies by pressing your thumb or the back of a teaspoon into the center of each; remove to wire racks to cool completely. Dust plain cookies with sifted powdered sugar. Fill indentations with jam or lemon curd.

Store in layers separated by waxed paper in an airtight container in the refrigerator for up to 1 week. Makes 60 cookies. Hand delivery is recommended.

For Lemon Twists: Sprinkle additional granulated sugar on counter; roll 2-tablespoon (30 ml) portions of dough into 8-inch (20 cm) long rolls, using sugar to prevent sticking. Loop each rope back against itself; twist gently. Place 2 inches (5 cm) apart on ungreased baking sheets. Bake about 12 minutes or until set. Allow to cool for 1 minute on baking sheet and then remove to wire racks to cool completely.

Store in airtight containers at room temperature for up to 3 weeks. Makes 28 twists. Lemon Twists are good for shipping.

For Swedish Bars: Form dough into three 13 x 1 ½-inch (33 x 4 cm) ropes. With handle of wooden spoon, make a lengthwise depression about ½ inch (1 cm) deep down the center of each rope. Fill with jam; sprinkle finely chopped pistachios alongside jam. Bake about 24 minutes or until set. Cool slightly, then slice diagonally into 1-inch (2.5 cm) bars.

Store in airtight containers at room temperature for about 2 weeks. Makes 36 bars. These ship well as long as they are wrapped to keep the jam from sticking.

Make-Your-Own Bars

Make-Your-Own Bars

These easy-to-make bars were developed when I had leftover chocolate chips, white chocolate chips, dried cranberries and walnuts, but not enough of each to make any of my favorite recipes. I used a chocolate chip bar cookie recipe and just threw in all my leftovers, and the result was delicious. Since then I always bake a batch of these at the end of my Christmas baking to use up any leftover goodies. Trust me, this is preferable to saving them for next year! —Mimi

2¼ cups (560 ml) all-purpose flour

1¼ teaspoons (6 ml) baking powder

¼ teaspoon (1 ml) salt

1 cup (250 ml) butter, softened

1¼ cup (60 ml) granulated sugar

1 large egg

1 teaspoon (5 ml) vanilla extract

3 cups (750 ml) of chips, nuts, and/or dried fruit (see suggestions below)

Pre-heat oven to 350°F (180°C). Grease a 9 x 13-inch (23 x 32 cm) baking pan. In a small bowl, combine the flour, baking powder, and salt; set aside. In a large mixing bowl, beat butter and sugar until creamy. Beat in egg and vanilla extract. Gradually blend in flour mixture. Stir in your preferred chips, nuts, and or dried fruit. Press into bottom of pan.

Bake 20 to 30 minutes. Baking for 20 minutes will result in a chewier cookie and 30 minutes will give you a crispier cookie. Cool completely. Cut into 2-inch (5 cm) squares.

Store in an airtight container at room temperature for up to 1 month. Makes 30 bars. These are great shippers!

Suggestions:
- 2 cups (500 ml) semi-sweet chocolate chips and 1 cup (250 ml) chopped walnuts
- 2 cups (500 ml) white chocolate chips and 1 cup (250 ml) chopped macadamia nuts
- 1 cup (250 ml) white chocolate chips, 1 cup (250 ml) chopped walnuts, and 1 cup (250 ml) dried cranberries
- 2 cups (500 ml) butterscotch chips and 1 cup (250 ml) chopped pecans
- 1½ (375 ml) cups chopped pecans and 1½ (375 ml) cups chopped dried apricots

Cherry Chewbilees

Cherry Chewbilees

Here is another festive update to the chocolate chip cookie, courtesy of the Cherry Marketing Institute.

1 cup (250 ml) margarine, softened

¾ cup (175 ml) granulated sugar

¾ cup (175 ml) brown sugar, firmly packed

2 large eggs

1 teaspoon (5 ml) vanilla extract

2¼ cups (560 ml) all-purpose flour

1 teaspoon (5 ml) baking soda

1⅔ cups (400 ml) coarsely chopped white chocolate or vanilla milk chips

1½ cups (375 ml) dried tart cherries

1 cup (250 ml) cashews, coarsely chopped

Pre-heat oven to 350°F (180°C). Combine margarine, granulated sugar, brown sugar, eggs and vanilla in a large mixing bowl. Beat with an electric mixer on medium speed until thoroughly mixed. Combine flour and baking soda; gradually add flour mixture to margarine mixture. Stir in white chocolate, dried cherries and cashews. Drop by rounded tablespoonfuls (15 ml) onto ungreased baking sheets. Bake 10 to 12 minutes, or until light golden brown. Do not overbake. Allow to cool for 1 minute on baking sheet, then remove to wire racks to cool completely.

Store in an airtight container at room temperature for up to 3 weeks. Makes 54 cookies. These cookies ship well.

photo courtesy of the California Walnut Commission

Walnut Cappuccino Biscotti

A coffee-lover's dream, these biscotti are perfect for dipping in your favorite hot beverage on cold winter nights. Recipe courtesy of the California Walnut Commission.

3 large eggs

2 tablespoons (30 ml) extra-virgin olive oil

⅛ cup (30 ml) whole milk

1 cup (250 ml) granulated sugar

¼ cup (60 ml) brown sugar

2½ cups (625 ml) all-purpose flour

2 tablespoons (30 ml) cocoa powder

1 teaspoon (5 ml) baking soda

4 teaspoons (20 ml) coffee beans ground for espresso

1 cup (250 ml) toasted California walnuts, chopped

Pre-heat the oven to 350°F (180°C). In a mixer bowl using a paddle attachment, mix all of the ingredients until a sticky dough is formed.

Place dough onto a floured surface. Divide evenly into two pieces. Roll the dough into two 12-inch (30 cm) logs. Place on a parchment-lined or greased baking sheet and pat the logs down flat—approximately 3½ inches (9 cm) wide. Bake the logs until they spring back when pressed lightly.

Allow the logs to cool, then using a bread knife, cut into biscotti about ½ inch (1.5 cm) thick. Arrange the biscotti on the baking sheet, flat on their side. Bake again, at 350°F (180°C), for 8 more minutes. Let cool.

Store in an airtight container at room temperature for up to 1 month. Makes 48 biscotti. Perfect for shipping.

photo courtesy of the Cranberry Marketing Committee

Healthy Cranberry Thumbprint Cookies

Healthy Cranberry Thumbprint Cookies

The holidays don't have to be fattening. This delicious cookie—filled with spicy cranberry compote—will satisfy any sweet tooth without the extra fat! Recipe courtesy of the Cranberry Marketing Committee

Spicy Cranberry Orange filling:

12 ounces (340 g) fresh cranberries

2 oranges, peeled and chopped

1 cup (250 ml) granulated sugar

½ teaspoon (5 ml) ground cinnamon

¼ teaspoon (1 ml) ground nutmeg

⅛ teaspoon (0.5 ml) ground cloves

2 teaspoons (10 ml) grated orange zest

low-fat thumbprint cookie:

4 to 4½ cups (1 *l* to 1.25 *l*) all-purpose flour

¼ cup (60 ml) hazelnuts, toasted and diced

1 teaspoon (5 ml) ground cinnamon

¾ teaspoon (4 ml) baking soda

¼ teaspoon (1 ml) salt

1¼ cups (310 ml) granulated sugar

¼ cup (60 ml) butter or margarine

1 large egg

1 egg white

1 teaspoon (5 ml) vanilla extract

⅔ cup (150 ml) applesauce

For the filling, place cranberries, oranges, sugar and spices in medium saucepan. Cover and bring to a boil. Turn down heat and simmer 12 to 15 minutes, stirring occasionally, until cranberries burst and mixture is the consistency of jam. Remove from heat and stir in orange peel; set aside.

For the cookies, pre-heat oven to 375°F (190°C). Grease baking sheets. Stir flour, hazelnuts, cinnamon, baking soda and salt together; set aside. Beat sugar and butter or margarine together until creamy. Add egg, egg white and vanilla. Beat until light and fluffy. Add applesauce and beat until blended. Beating on low speed, slowly add flour mixture to creamed mixture. Beat until just blended. Cover and chill in refrigerator 1 to 2 hours. Shape dough into 1-inch (2.5 cm) balls and place on prepared baking sheet. Flatten dough into 3-inch (8 cm) circle with bottom of glass.* Using thumb, make a wide indentation on top of each cookie. Place 1 teaspoon (5 ml) filling into each center. Bake for 8 to 12 minutes until edges are lightly browned. Allow to cool 1 minute on baking sheet, then remove to wire racks to cool completely.

Store between sheets of waxed paper in an airtight container at room temperature for up to 3 weeks. Makes about 42 cookies. These cookies should be hand-delivered.

* If glass sticks to dough, dip glass in sugar before flattening dough.

Speculaci: German Christmas Cookies

Speculaci: German Christmas Cookies

This recipe was submitted by Johanne Bezaire, whose story can be found on page 182. Johanne's recipe comes from an old 1920s cookbook. She says, "It takes a little practice to get the right consistency: with too little flour the edges of the cookies blur when baked; too much and they're tough and lacking in flavor." She adds that if you are unsure, cut out a couple of cookies and test them. We found that it's important to actually use a spoon to mix the dough as directed, because an electric stand mixer incorporates too much flour. Make sure to read Johanne's story for more info on how to decorate these cookies.

1 cup (250 ml) butter, softened

1 cup (250 ml) granulated sugar

1 cup (250 ml) brown sugar, firmly packed

3 large eggs

1 teaspoon (5 ml) vanilla extract

all-purpose flour

Pre-heat oven to 350°F (180°C). Beat butter and sugar until light and fluffy, then beat in eggs and vanilla thoroughly. With a wooden spoon, stir in enough sifted flour to make a soft dough that pulls away from the side of the bowl when stirred. The amount needed will depend on the temperature and humidity in your kitchen. Wrap dough in plastic wrap and refrigerate about 1 hour.

On a lightly floured board, roll dough very thin and cut into shapes with cookie cutters. Place on an ungreased cookie sheet and bake about 12 minutes or until bottoms are lightly browned. Allow to cool for 2 minutes on the baking sheet, then remove to a wire rack to cool completely.

Store in an airtight container at room temperature for about 1 month if unfrosted or 1 week if frosted. Makes 36 to 48 cookies, depending on the size of the cookie cutters. These cookies ship well if cut into regular geometric shapes (such as circles or squares) and packed very carefully. They will most likely break if you cut them into irregular shapes like Santa Claus and snowflakes. If you want to use fancy cookie cutters, it is best to hand-deliver these cookies.

Grandma Helen's Chocolate Chip Cookies

Grandma Helen's Chocolate Chip Cookies

Eric R. Liscinsky sent us his mother's recipe for the perfect Chocolate Chip Cookie. We agree it's one of the best we've ever tasted! It's soft and chewy and delicious. Here's a hint: the bigger you make them and the less you bake them, the softer they will be. See Eric's charming story on page 176.

2¼ cups (560 ml) sifted all-purpose flour

1 teaspoon (5 ml) baking soda

1 teaspoon (5 ml) salt

1 cup (250 ml) solid vegetable shortening, butter-flavored

¾ cup (175 ml) granulated sugar

¾ cup (175 ml) brown sugar, firmly packed

2 large eggs

1 teaspoon (5 ml) vanilla extract

½ teaspoon (2 ml) water

2 cups (500 ml) semi-sweet chocolate chips

1 cup (250 ml) chopped nuts (optional)

Pre-heat oven to 375°F (190°C). In a medium bowl, sift together flour, baking soda, and salt. Set aside. In a large bowl beat shortening, granulated sugar, and brown sugar until light and fluffy. Beat in eggs; add vanilla and water. Gradually add flour mixture; mix well. Stir in chocolate chips and nuts.

Drop by teaspoons (5 ml) on a greased or non-stick baking sheet. Bake 10 to 12 minutes or until set and slightly brown. Allow to cool for 1 minute on baking sheet and then remove to a wire rack to cool completely.

Store in a cookie jar at room temperature for about 1 month. Makes 60 cookies. Chocolate chip cookies are one of the best cookies to ship.

Loretta Painter's Soft Sugar Cookies with Royal Icing

Loretta Painter's Soft Sugar Cookies

This is the fabulous recipe that saved Christmas in Dorene Sparks' story "A Silk Purse Christmas" found on page 174. Loretta Painter owns a restaurant and catering business in Dorene's hometown of Stewardson, Illinois. Dorene says that using margarine rather than butter keeps the cookies softer longer. We've found that if you under-bake them by a couple minutes, they are even softer!

1 cup (250 ml) margarine

1½ cup (375 ml) granulated sugar

2 large eggs

¾ cup (175 ml) sour cream

1 teaspoon (5 ml) vanilla extract

1 teaspoon (5 ml) baking soda

1 teaspoon (5 ml) baking powder

½ teaspoon (2 ml) salt

4 cups (1 *l*) all-purpose flour

In a large mixing bowl, mix well all ingredients except flour. Gradually stir in the flour about a cup at a time until well incorporated. Dough will be soft. Wrap dough in plastic wrap and chill for several hours or overnight, until it has firmed up.

Pre-heat oven to 350°F (180°C). On a floured board, roll dough out to about ¼ inch (½ cm) thick and cut into shapes with floured cookie cutters.

Place on ungreased baking sheets and bake about 15 minutes or until edges are slightly browned. Let cool about 1 minute on the baking sheet and then remove to wire rack to cool completely. Decorate with your favorite icing. Dorene uses a mixture of powdered sugar and milk, stirring until she achieves the consistency that she wants. We like Royal Icing; recipe follows.

Store in an airtight container at room temperature for up to 1 month if not frosted or up to 1 week if frosted. Makes approximately 48 cookies, depending on the size cookie cutters you use. These cookies ship well if cut into regular geometric shapes (such as circles or squares) and packed very carefully. They can break during shipping if you cut them into irregular or delicate shapes like Santa Claus and snowflakes. If you want to use fancy cookie cutters, it is best to hand-deliver these cookies.

Royal Icing

This is our favorite icing for Sugar Cookies. It dries hard and glossy so it is less messy and more durable for gift-giving than creamy frosting. We recommend you do not use raw egg whites in this recipe. If you cannot find pasteurized egg whites (the kind that come in a little milk carton) in your grocery store, you can use 5 tablespoons (75 ml) powdered egg whites or meringue powder. Just increase the amount of water.

1 pound (500 g) powdered sugar
¼ cup (60 ml) pasteurized egg whites
2 tablespoons (30 ml) water, as needed
food coloring (optional)

Combine powdered sugar and meringue powder or egg whites in a mixing bowl and beat on low speed. Add water drop by drop. Depending on the temperature and humidity in your kitchen you may not need to add all the water. Beat until the mixture holds a ribbon-like trail on the surface for five seconds when you raise the mixer from the bowl.

If desired, separate icing into several different bowls and add food coloring to each bowl to make different colors of icing. Decorate cookies by spreading the icing on the cookie with an offset spatula or a butter knife, or by placing the icing in a pastry bag with a small round tip and piping the icing onto the cookies. If you do not have a pastry bag, just place the icing in a resealable plastic bag and snip off a very small corner.

Store in an airtight container in the refrigerator for up to 1 week. Makes 3 cups (750 ml). Cookies decorated with this icing should not be stored for more than 1 week because the icing tends to crystallize and doesn't look as smooth and glossy, although it remains safe to eat.

"Ashtray" Sugar Cookies

"Ashtray" Sugar Cookies

This recipe is from Lynn Kopsie and her mother, Nancy Stola. The cookies got their name because when Lynn was a child they used a new ashtray with a pretty design stamped into the bottom to decorate the cookies. We like them because they are pretty but simple to make. Read the rest of Lynn's story on page 178.

3 cups (750 ml) all-purpose flour

2 teaspoons (10 ml) baking powder

1 teaspoon (5 ml) baking soda

½ teaspoon (2 ml) salt

1 cup (250 ml) butter, cold

2 large eggs

1 cup (250 ml) granulated sugar

1 teaspoon (5 ml) vanilla

Pre-heat oven to 350°F (180°C). Sift together flour, baking powder, baking soda, and salt. Cut in butter until mixture resembles fine crumbs. Beat together eggs, sugar, and vanilla. Stir into flour mixture. Mix well and shape into walnut-size balls. Place on greased baking sheet.

Press each cookie with an object that has a base with a pretty design, such as a glass, vase, or clean ashtray dipped in granulated sugar. Bake 8 to 10 minutes or until light brown. Allow to cool 1 minute on the baking sheet and then remove to wire rack to cool.

Store in an airtight container at room temperature for up to 1 month. Makes about 36 cookies. These cookies ship well.

Old-Fashioned Oatmeal Cookies

This recipe is from Lynn Kopsie and her mother, Nancy Stola, who made them when Lynn was a child. Lynn says, "Using goose fat in these oatmeal cookies was exceptional! The cookies melted in your mouth and everyone agreed they were the best they ever ate." See the rest of Lynn's story on page 178.

Goose fat is prized in European cooking. It is the healthiest of all animal fats, containing less saturated fat and more of the good mono- and poly-unsaturated fats. You can find it at gourmet food stores, European specialty stores, and sometimes at your local butcher shop.

2 cups (500 ml) sifted all-purpose flour

1 teaspoon (5 ml) baking soda

1 teaspoon (5 ml) salt

1½ teaspoon (375 ml) cinnamon

2 cups (500 ml) quick cooking oatmeal

½ cup (125 ml) brown sugar, firmly packed

½ cup (125 ml) granulated sugar

1 cup (250 ml) rendered goose fat

2 large eggs

⅓ cup (75 ml) milk or sour milk

1 teaspoon (5 ml) vanilla

1 cup (250 ml) raisins, or chopped dates or figs

1 cup (250 ml) chopped nuts or chocolate morsels

Pre-heat oven to 350°F (180°C). Grease 2 baking sheets. In a large bowl, sift together flour, baking soda, salt, and cinnamon. Stir in oats, brown sugar, granulated sugar, goose fat, eggs, milk, and vanilla. Mix until well blended. Add raisins and nuts and mix well.

Drop by teaspoonfuls (5 ml) onto baking sheets and bake about 12 minutes or until brown. Remove from oven and cool on baking sheet about 1 minute. Remove to a wire rack to cool completely.

Store in airtight containers in the refrigerator for up to 3 weeks. Makes about 60 cookies. These cookies ship well.

Peanut Butter Blossoms

This recipe was contributed by Karen Sloper, whose story can be read on page 165. "Peanut Blossoms" first appeared as a Pillsbury Bake-Off® winner in 1957. Since then they have become a perennial Christmas favorite and many people have made their own adaptations to the recipe. Here is Karen's family's favorite.

48 foil-wrapped milk chocolate pieces, unwrapped (about 1 8-ounce or 225g bag)

½ cup (125 ml) solid vegetable shortening, butter flavored

¾ cup (175 ml) peanut butter

⅓ cup (75 ml) granulated sugar

⅓ cup (75 ml) light brown sugar, firmly packed

1 large egg

2 tablespoons (30 ml) milk

1 teaspoon (5 ml) vanilla extract

1½ cup (375 ml) all-purpose flour

1 teaspoon (5 ml) baking soda

½ teaspoon (2 ml) salt

additional granulated sugar

Pre-heat oven to 375°F (190°C). In large bowl, beat shortening and peanut butter. Add ⅓ cup (75 ml) granulated sugar and brown sugar; beat until light and fluffy. Add egg, milk, and vanilla; beat well. Stir together flour, baking soda and salt; gradually stir into peanut butter mixture. Shape dough into 1-inch (2.5 cm) balls, then roll each ball in additional granulated sugar.

Place on ungreased baking sheet and bake 8 to 10 minutes or until lightly browned. Immediately place chocolate kiss on top of each cookie, pressing down firmly so cookie cracks around edges. Remove from baking sheet to wire rack to cool completely.

Store in an airtight container at room temperature for about 1 month. Makes about 48 cookies. These ship well.

Divinity

Divinity

Laurie Turner, whose story is on page 169, shared this recipe with us. Laurie recommends using clear vanilla to keep the candy whiter, and to use a candy thermometer to make sure the syrup reaches the correct temperature. She adds that using a heavy-duty stand mixer is a big plus. It's best to have two people spooning out the candy at the same time to get all the pieces made before the candy starts to harden.

3 egg whites, beaten until stiff peaks form

4 cups (1ℓ) granulated sugar

1 cup (250 ml) light corn syrup

¾ (175 ml) cup water

1 teaspoon (5 ml) vanilla

chopped or whole nuts (optional)

Bring sugar, syrup, and water to a boil; boil until hard ball stage, 250°F to 268°F (121°C to 131°C). Add boiled mixture to beaten egg whites very slowly, beating constantly until it just starts to lose its gloss. Stir in vanilla and nuts. The candy is done when it forms peaks when you lift the mixer. Test often to avoid over-beating the mixture.

Quickly spoon onto waxed paper, forming a peak on the top of each piece. If desired, top with nuts. Allow to cool and harden.

Store in airtight container at room temperature for up to 1 month. Makes approximately 48 walnut-sized pieces. This candy ships well.

Christmas Cookie
Gift Presentation

Christmas Cookie Gift Presentation

WHEN HAND-DELIVERING your gift of Christmas cookies, you should make your gift look as impressive as it tastes. If the cookies you've made are of a type that doesn't keep long, give them freshly baked. You can give certain cookies such as Springerle or Pfeffernuesse (there is a good recipe at Christmas-Cookies.com) some time after baking them, since they can be baked a month beforehand and allowed to mellow to perfection.

Choose a decorative and sturdy container to put the cookies in. Examples can be new or vintage cookie tins, cookie jars, decorative vases or bowls, pretty hatboxes, or a large 2-quart (2 *ℓ*) mason jar tied with a pretty ribbon. Handle the container with care until delivered. If you think the cookies might be jostled around in transit, our tips for shipping cookies may apply (see page 145). Anyone would be delighted to receive such a thoughtful and delicious homemade gift. However, if you want your gift to be more attractive and elaborate, you can take it much further.

One idea might be to create an entire cookie basket with your home-baked cookies as the *pièce de résistance*. With your cookies in their container, give your friends the recipe handwritten on some pretty paper or printed out with a fancy font, and place some of the equipment necessary to bake the cookies in the basket, such as:

- a set of copper cookie cutters
- a rolling pin
- a wooden mixing spoon

- a large mixing bowl
- a new baking pan
- a set of quality stainless steel measuring cups
- a mason jar filled with the dry ingredients in the recipe (see "Gifts in a Jar," page 151)

You could also add some things that go well with your cookies, such as:

- sachets of hot chocolate or instant cappuccino
- a set of pretty coffee mugs or teacups
- a pretty coffee or tea pot
- attractive napkins
- a decorative cookie plate
- a copy of this book

Another idea is to bake a batch of cookies from a recipe in this book, such as The Giving Christmas Cookie (page 32) or the Easy Triple Chocolate Caramel Brownies (page 96), and wrap it in a basket with a copy of the book.

If you put a little extra thought and care into packaging your homemade cookies, your gift will be sure to be the hit of the Christmas party.

Shipping
Christmas Cookies

Shipping Christmas Cookies

THE THREE MOST IMPORTANT FACTORS to consider when deciding to send Christmas cookies to someone far away are:

- ❧ What kind of cookies you bake
- ❧ How you package them
- ❧ How you ship them

The Cookie That Doesn't Crumble

Select cookies that are soft or moist. Brittle, crispy, or delicate cookies could break and crumble in transit. Bar cookies and drop cookies are the best shippers. Select only cookies that will keep for 2 weeks or more, depending upon the approximate shipping time to the recipient. Cookies with moist fillings do not make good shippers because the fillings can get squeezed out and make a sticky mess. Do not send cookies frosted with soft frosting, either, as the frosting will rub off during transit.

Crispy or odd shaped cookies such as shortbread, cutout sugar cookies or gingerbread cookies break easily, and their different shapes make them hard to pack. That said, it can be done if you take the time to pack them very carefully. Small geometric shapes are less likely to break than large irregular ones.

The Christmas Box

Select a nice presentation box for your cookies. This can be a vintage cookie or candy tin, a hatbox, a shoebox that your children have decorated, or any clean, attractive, and sturdy container.

Pack the cookies properly by wrapping them together in short stacks of 5 or 6 using plastic wrap. Do not wrap different types of cookies together because the flavors will transfer from one to the other and none will taste right. Place the wrapped stacks inside the container in snug rows lined with bubble wrap or crumpled tissue paper. Place more bubble wrap or tissue paper between each layer of cookies. Make sure that there is plenty of packing material inside your container so that the cookies don't move around. They should be snugly secure but not squeezed in tight. If you shake the box and they don't move around, you will know that they are secure enough to survive the rigors of travel.

You can also bake bar cookies inside a disposable foil pan and send them pan and all. Just wrap the pan well with plastic wrap.

Place your cookie container inside a larger cardboard box for mailing. Make sure that packing material surrounds the container on all sides to prevent it from getting crushed in case the outer box is damaged in transit. Do not use real popcorn (the kind you eat) as packing material because this could get moldy if the box gets wet in transit—a likely situation in winter. Popcorn can also attract insects and rodents. Plastic foam peanuts are better. You can also use wadded-up newspaper or gift-wrap.

Special Delivery from Santa

When shipping Christmas cookies, plan to send them a little earlier than you normally would because of the extra delay that the post office experiences during the holiday season. Consider other options such as FedEx to ensure that your cookies arrive in time. If you ship them well ahead of time, you can put a note in the box telling your recipient that the cookies can be frozen until they are to be eaten, and to defrost them at room temperature for about 20 minutes before serving. Your cookies will already be properly wrapped for freezing, and you will have already chosen and baked cookies that keep well, so the recipient can just pop the whole box into the freezer.

Make sure that you properly address your package so that your cookies arrive at the correct destination in a timely fashion. Writing "Perishable" on the box may encourage more expedient handling. If you can afford the extra expense, ship your cookies via an overnight courier so that they will be as fresh as possible.

For domestic delivery, if you don't wish to ship the cookies overnight, send them airmail and not surface or ground. If you are shipping from one country to another, you must ship them via an express courier or they could take weeks or even months to arrive, depending on their ultimate destination. Remember to properly fill out the customs form on an international package or it will be returned to you. On this form, make sure to specify that it is a gift or your recipient could be charged customs duty for it. You wouldn't want them to have to pay for their own gift.

Planning ahead when you're shipping your cookies makes a more pleasant holiday for everyone, and ensures your gift will be well received.

Gifts in a Jar

Gifts in a Jar

Think you're too busy to make homemade gifts this year? Or maybe your recipient is too busy to bake? "Cookies in a Jar" mixes are a great idea for a thoughtful homemade gift that will be appreciated by everyone. These are standard 1-quart (1ℓ) mason jars filled with the ingredients to a cookie recipe placed in distinct layers that make a pretty horizontal stripe pattern. Sometimes these are referred to as "sand art" cookies because the jars resemble the handicrafts of that name.

To bake the cookies, your recipient need only follow the simple instructions printed on a card attached to the jar. Usually this involves mixing the contents of the jar with butter, an egg, and vanilla extract and then baking the cookies in the oven. Pretty, easy, and delicious—and hand made by you just for them! What could be better?

If you'd like to decorate your gift more creatively or stylishly, make a whole gift basket out of it that looks like it was done by a professional gift basket maker. Bake a batch of the cookies and put them in a cellophane bag tied with a ribbon. Then, using the same recipe as the cookies you made, create a "gift in a jar" by layering the ingredients in a mason jar. Tie that with a ribbon with the directions for making the cookies attached. Print up the original recipe on a card for them to keep, and round out the gift basket with a large mixing bowl, a wooden spoon, and any other item needed to make the cookies such as a cookie cutter or cookie press. Top it off with a cookie cookbook (this one would be perfect). Place all this in a large basket and wrap the basket with cellophane. Tie a fancy bow around the basket, and your gift is ready to give.

While these gifts are very simple to make, there are a few rules to follow to make them work properly. Here are some tips on how to make your gifts in a jar tasty and beautiful.

- ❧ Start with the freshest ingredients. Your gift in a jar will have a shelf life of 3 months in most cases. If you use fresh ingredients, they will keep that long and still taste delicious.

- ❧ To keep each layer separate and distinct, layer the ingredients properly to prevent the different layers sifting down into each other. Unless otherwise directed by your recipe, place the ingredients with the finest grains at the bottom, then add ingredients with larger grains, and finally top them off with any large chunks. Pack down each layer tightly before adding the next layer. Also, your gift will look prettier if you layer light and dark-colored ingredients alternately. Usually, your layers will go something like this depending on the ingredients:

  - **Bottom:** flour, cocoa powder
  - **Middle:** white sugar
  - **Middle:** oatmeal, ground nuts
  - **Middle:** brown sugar (its more sticky consistency works well as a base for large pieces)
  - **Top:** chopped nuts, chocolate chips, raisins, candy pieces

- ❧ If powdery substances such as cocoa powder or flour stick to the inside of the jar, wipe it down before adding the next layer.

- ❧ A small meat mallet or the end of a French rolling pin (without handles) works well as a tool to tamp down ingredients in the jar.

- ❧ If layering the ingredients seems like too much of a hassle, just put all the ingredients in the jar and give it a good shake!

- ❧ Dress up the jar. Take some pretty fabric and cut out a 9-inch (23 cm) circle with pinking shears. Place the circle on the lid of the jar and secure it around the neck of the jar using raffia or a ribbon. Print out the instructions on fancy paper using a decorative font and tie the instructions to the jar.

- ❧ On the printed card, add the shelf life of the ingredients (usually about 3 months), as well as instructions to keep the jar in a cool, dark place. Your recipient will be assured of tasty cookies even if he or she can't get around to making them right away.

Where do you find recipes for cookies in a jar? There are many at Christmas-Cookies.com, but you can turn your favorite recipes into "Gifts in a Jar" as long as the total of dry ingredients is 1 quart (1 ℓ) or less. You may have to cut your current recipe by half or one third to get the correct amount of dry ingredients, but it will work. Remember to adjust the amounts of wet ingredients needed when writing out your directions to place on the jar. Or, rather than cutting your recipe, you can use the larger 2-quart (2 ℓ) mason jars, and if there is any space left at the top of the jar, pack it tightly with tissue paper or add a few extra nuts or chocolate chips—this adds pizzazz!

To get you started, we're providing you with two of our favorite Cookies in a Jar recipes. We think they're pretty, and they taste great.

Chocolate Chip Cookies in a Jar

Chocolate Chip Cookies in a Jar

1⅔ cups (400 ml) all-purpose flour

¾ teaspoon (3 ml) baking soda

½ cup (125 ml) granulated sugar

½ cup (125 ml) light brown sugar, firmly packed

1 cup (250 ml) semi-sweet chocolate chips

1 cup (250 ml) chopped walnuts or pecans

Sift together the flour and the baking soda, then place in the bottom of a 1-quart (1 *l*) glass mason jar. Tamp down the flour so it is packed in firmly. Add the rest of the ingredients in this order, making sure to pack down each ingredient as you add it: granulated sugar, brown sugar, semi-sweet chocolate chips, chopped nuts. Screw the lid on the jar. Attach the following directions:

Chocolate Chip Cookies

Note: Store this jar in a cool, dark place for up to 3 months before using.

contents of this jar

¾ cup (175 ml) butter, softened

1 large egg plus 1 egg yolk

1 teaspoon (5 ml) vanilla extract

Pre-heat oven to 375°F (190°C). Empty the contents of the jar into a medium bowl. In a large bowl beat together butter, eggs, and vanilla until creamy. Gradually stir in dry ingredients. Drop by tablespoonfuls (15 ml) onto an ungreased cookie sheet and bake 8 to 10 minutes. Remove from oven and let cool for 1 minute, then remove the cookies to a wire rack to cool completely. Store in an airtight container at room temperature for up to 3 weeks. Makes 24 cookies.

Oatmeal Raisin Spice Cookies in a Jar

1 cup (250 ml) all-purpose flour

1 teaspoon (5 ml) ground cinnamon

½ teaspoon (2 ml) ground nutmeg

1 teaspoon (5 ml) baking soda

½ teaspoon (2 ml) salt

½ cup (125 ml) granulated sugar

¾ cup (175 ml) dark brown sugar, firmly packed

2 cups (500 ml) quick cooking oatmeal

¾ cup (175 ml) raisins

Sift together flour, ground cinnamon, ground nutmeg, baking soda and salt, then place in the bottom of a 1-quart (1 *l*) glass mason jar. Tamp down the flour mixture so it is packed in firmly. Add the rest of the ingredients in the order given, making sure to pack down each layer firmly before adding the next. Screw the lid on the jar. Attach the following directions:

Oatmeal Raisin Spice Cookies

Note: Store this jar in a cool, dark place for up to 3 months before using.

contents of this jar
¾ cup (175 ml) butter or margarine, softened

1 large egg, slightly beaten
1 teaspoon (5 ml) vanilla extract

Pre-heat oven to 350°F (175°C). Line two baking sheets with parchment paper. Empty the jar of cookie mix into a large mixing bowl, blend the mixture thoroughly. Stir in butter or margarine, egg, and vanilla. Mix until completely blended. Shape into balls the size of walnuts. Place 2 inches (5 cm) apart on prepared baking sheets. Bake for 11 to 13 minutes or until edges are lightly browned. Let cool for 5 minutes and then transfer to a wire rack to cool completely. Store in an airtight container at room temperature for up to 3 weeks. Makes 36 cookies.

Christmas Cookie Stories

Susan J. Talbutt
Wyncote, Pennsylvania

Good marriages are based on trust, respect, shared interests and friendship. My marriage is also based on Springerle—those anise-flavored, sculptural, German cookies. And because they become rock-hard when stale, they do make a solid foundation.

My German-born grandmother had taught me how to make Springerle one Christmas while I was still in college. Using my mother's new mixer, she showed me how to beat the eggs until they had reached maximum volume, then to slowly add the flour by hand. While the dough rested, we cleaned the kitchen. After an hour, she carefully pressed her mother's mold—warped by years of washing in hot water—into the sticky dough and cut the cookies apart with a very sharp knife. Again and again we rolled fresh dough and scraps. The last bit of dough she shaped by hand into a small square and pressed a corner of the mold onto it.

Always preferring cooking to baking, Mom was happy to give me her 25-year-old mixer the next Christmas so that I could bake in my new apartment in West Virginia. My food-loving boyfriend was more than happy to help with the project during his visit. He was so looking forward to those anise-flavored squares!

Dutifully, I followed Grandma's handwritten directions, beating the eggs and sugar on high speed for half an hour. The mixer, however, wasn't up to the job, and slowed down and smoked after about 20 or 25 minutes. We turned it off, let it rest, and finished the rest of the recipe by hand. The mixer made it through the remaining recipes, but was never the same again. The cookies were a success. Springerle were now my sweetie's favorite cookies.

The next holiday season found me still in West Virginia, still with the same Springerle-loving boyfriend, still with no mixer. There was a backup plan. Germans in the Stuttgart area baked Springerle long before the invention of household appliances. It was Grandma's father's job to beat the eggs and sugar for about an hour. Well, we would simply trade off beating the eggs every ten minutes or so.

My sweetie, faced with the prospect of no cookies or hours of hand mixing, took matters into his own hands.

During my visit home for Thanksgiving, he brought me into his apartment and told me he had bought my Christmas present early. On the floor was a largish box wrapped in newspaper. My heart beat faster and my mouth grew dry. Only an appliance would be in a box of that size.

I ripped that paper off with glee! Oh wonder of wonders! A KitchenAid 4½ quart stand mixer! My dream mixer! A mixer I hadn't expected to own until marriage—a far-off event in misty future. A mixer I couldn't afford and had drooled over!

He had bought it at our favorite kitchenware store, where we had our first "date" and had browsed the aisles for three hours. (I bought a fry pan, an apron, and a quarter pound of Ceylon tea. The tea is long gone but the fry pan and apron are still with me.) The store is in South Philadelphia, two miles from his apartment. With no car and little chance of catching a bus or taxi, he rode his bicycle the two miles with the mixer balanced in front of him on the bike's cross bar.

Later, my mother would say that the mixer is what told her he was serious. I have baked Springerle every year since then, even the year we were married nine days before Christmas.

Sue's wonderful Springerle recipe can be found on her website at http://www.christmas-baking.com/

Karen Sloper
Wilsonville, Oregon

This story is probably like most as far as traditions go. My children and I have baked treats each year—especially cookies for Santa and family. We usually bake Peanut Butter Blossoms and sugar cookies. We use cookie cutters for the sugar cookies (we have so many of them) and decorate them with frosting and sprinkles.

What has been more difficult is that I am now disabled and don't have a lot of energy to bake. I used to bake all the time before my illness. Now it is a rare and special occasion to do any baking because of my energy level and pain. Through this, it has become so much more special to bake cookies with my children during the holidays. It has also given me an opportunity to let go, and not worry if the cookies don't look just "right." My children are really learning how to bake because I'm not doing it all. I'm letting them pick the recipes, plan for ingredients and do the decorating. They love it because they're learning how to bake and understand recipes and what it means to put in a "tsp." or "tbsp." They also have such an appreciation for the love and care that goes into making something yourself. I am very proud of them and their interest and help. We are a team! My children's ages are 10, 8, and 4 years old. It's a lot of fun.

See Karen's recipe for Peanut Butter Blossoms on page 136.

Stephanie Marsh
Myrtle Creek, Oregon

My grandmother was a great lady not just to me but to all who knew her. All of her home-ec students, students whom she made home visits to even when it wasn't popular to do so, felt that she was very special. Then all of her and my grandfather's square dance students, students who later made it possible for the two of them to be voted as the Square Dance Couple of the Year, only the second time that the award was ever presented, also found her to be a spirited and lively lady with a good heart. Her genealogy students, clients, and peers, people that helped make it possible for her to later in life go to Russia in representation of the United States of America in attempting to persuade the Russians to open their genealogy records to our country, felt that she was highly intelligent and very persuasive.

Within our family, she was the glue, the place where the love began. When my numerous cousins and I were young, she would have us all over on one day shortly before Christmas. She would get out all the pots, pans, wooden spoons, and all the other paraphernalia it took to make cookies and candies. We would spend a good portion of the day making chocolate dipped candies, butter mints, fudge, and all sorts of cookies.

My favorites were always the Christmas cutout cookies. I loved choosing from all of the different cookie cutters that would be laying out just waiting for little hands to start using them after waiting an entire year from last being used. Grandma would then, oh so very carefully, lift all the cookies from the layer of dough after we had pressed as hard as our little hands would allow, and sometimes not enough, to make those lovely little shapes. She would move them to the cookie sheets, then bake them until they were just right.

It would seem forever before we could get to frost them since we had to wait for them to cool. When they were finally cool enough we would get to start the best part, making the frosting. Yummy! I never knew then, but I am sure now, that so many little fingers were dipping into that frosting when Grandma wasn't looking that we must have eaten half of what was made. We would put into the bowl all of the ingredients that Grandma told us to put in, powdered sugar, butter, eggs, vanilla, then the mixer would start with its one-of-a-kind scent of the motor going and the ingredients of the frosting. It would be mixed until fluffy and tasty. Then, one drop at a time, in went the different colors of food coloring into the separated bowls of frosting. We would each have a bowl and a spoon with Grandma watching closely in case someone decided to have a heavy hand with the food coloring. The frosting would slowly change into the wonderful colors of Christmas. Then the knives would be brought out for us to apply the frosting to the cooled cookies. The colored sugars and sprinkles would be available for us to use as well.

It's funny, those cookies, no matter how carefully I make them now, never look as beautiful to my eyes now as they did on those wonderful, warm, cozy, cookie scented days that we spent with Grandma.

Kelly Raney-Wilson
Somerville, Ohio

The day would start with the three of us, my little brother and sister and me, waking up and checking under the tree to see if there were any new additions! My mother would secretly add a present or two every day until Santa came. The announcement that it was time to make Christmas cookies would bring us rushing into the kitchen with bright eyes and way too much energy! I don't know how my mom did it, but she let us all help. The flour was everywhere; the smell of butter and sugar was in the air. Is there any sweeter smell? After rolling, cutting and baking, she would mix up several bowls of "paint" and break out the sprinkles, "silver balls," sugar crystals, and all sorts of decorating supplies. The table looked like kid heaven. We were not rushed, or criticized for our purple Santas or pink trees. We created what we thought were masterpieces. And our mother made sure we felt like the greatest painters ever. We laughed, told stories, had hot chocolate, and made the most beautiful memories while painting those cookies. But the love we took with us from that kitchen table is what brings us back every year. Thirty years later and we still get together to paint Christmas cookies, only now we bring our own kids to the greatest kitchen table in the world.

Laurie Turner
Cannon Falls, Minnesota

When I was little, my mom always made trays of cookies for special people for the holidays. I remember helping and thinking that it was a lot of work, especially when each tray was made to have those special treats that that specific person enjoyed. She used to make Divinity for my grandpa; it was one of his favorites. In fact, he usually received an extra package that was put away just for him. As I got older, I began to make Divinity for him, then my dad, then my brother. Now I get requests for different items—Divinity, fudge, etc. One of my best friends taught me to can, so now these trays often contain jars of jelly or jam, breads or muffins. Once when canning, I forgot what type of jelly I made and labeled it "Mystery Jelly." I still get requests for that kind—it was blackberry jelly. I have found out how pleasurable it is to make something myself and give it to someone who enjoys it and look forward to planning what I will put on the trays. I know I have enjoyed these types of gifts when I was the recipient.

Laurie generously shared her Divinity recipe with us; see page 138.

Maureen Yin
King of Prussia, Pennsylvania

I added a word to the dictionary during the Christmas holidays—MomMom's Sugar Cookies: dough rolled out thinly on floured surface and cut with assorted Christmas shapes together with fun, laughter and love. Although MomMom has moved to heaven, as I roll and cut the same recipe along with the same cookie cutters, in the same kitchen where the tradition started, the memories are etched in my thoughts. Thoughts of love and caring and MomMom's great smile with the bright twinkle of her eyes as she baked the best tasting sugar cookies ever made—in my book, my dictionary! Thank you, MomMom!

Rita Cummins
Las Vegas, Nevada

In 1979 business affairs made it necessary for my husband and me to divide our time between offices in Michigan and those in California. Since our 9-year-old daughter was in school, she needed to stay in one place. On our returning to California after an extended stay in Michigan, she surprised us. Instead of being ecstatically happy at seeing her parents again, she threw a tantrum—over nothing! When she got over that, she did it again. I thought, what is wrong with this child? Then I realized that she felt neglected. What she needed was not discipline but quality time with her parents. What better way, with a 9-year-old girl, than baking cookies? So out came the recipe book. Out came the mixing bowl and the rolling pin. Soon tantrums were replaced with dusty hands and floury smiles. The following year we were able to resolve our business difficulties and live together as a family again, but in '79 the cookies saved us!

Cindy Robert
Kissimmee, Florida

While growing up, baking cookies was as much a part of Christmas time for me as tinsel and pine needles. Every year, a few weeks before Christmas, my mom (with my help) would start making a variety of delicious cookies. Smells of cinnamon and other spices enticed the whole family to "visit" the kitchen with much more frequency than usual. When the last cookie had finally cooled she would carefully wrap them and give them to me to place in lunch bags that I had decorated. It was a sight to see our dining room table covered from end to end with ribbon and crayon bedecked brown bags! They didn't stay around long though; they were soon distributed to various friends, neighbors, teachers, paperboys, the mailman, and anyone who happened to stop by.

I'm not sure when Mom quit baking all those cookies every year. I would hazard a guess that it was the year I announced that I was too old to scribble pictures of Santa Claus and Christmas trees on lunch sacks. Or maybe it was when I was too busy to help pass out the tasty gifts. To be honest, I didn't even notice. I hadn't thought about the Christmas cookie tradition until just the other day when my five year old daughter, Grace, asked if she could use some cookie cutters to shape her Play-Doh with.

I'd bought them years before meaning to try my hand at sugar cookies. But I'd gotten busy with other things and they'd gotten pushed into the back of a drawer where they'd been promptly forgotten. I explained to Grace what they were for and suggested maybe we could use them to bake some cookies at Christmas time. She asked if we could make enough so her whole kindergarten class could have some.

I thought that was a wonderful idea and am planning on getting some lunch bags for us to pack them in!

Dorene Sparks
Stewardson, Illinois

My mother-in-law always used to use the phrase "making a silk purse out of a sow's ear." I had to do that one Christmas.

My daughter was 3 years old. We had lived away from my home town for a couple of years. We had just moved back a few months before winter to try to get a fresh start. My husband had lost his job and we were struggling just to make ends meet. I didn't know what we would do for Christmas that year. We scrimped and saved to have some money to buy a present or two for our beautiful little girl, but knew we would have no money to buy anything for anyone else, not even each other.

I came up with a crazy idea. My husband thought I had lost my mind but said at least we wouldn't go to Christmas dinner empty handed. I decided to have a Tupperware party and use the money or points to buy containers for baked goods. Then, I purchased flour, sugar, nuts, chocolate chips and other baking ingredients with some of my food stamp money. I asked the mother of a good friend of mine, who makes the best cookies in the world, if she would share some of her famous recipes with me. She eagerly did. With containers in hand and my ingredients, my 3 year old and I went to work. We baked for 2 days.

When we were finished, we tied our containers with pretty bows just like a package and went to our Christmas dinners with gifts in hand. She was so proud to tell each guest that she had helped mommy bake their presents. Each gift was received with love and lots of compliments.

My daughter is now 15, and remembering that Christmas years ago always reminds me that Christmas is not about giving but about celebrating the birth of Jesus. The size or cost of the gift is unimportant when the gift is from the heart.

Loretta Painter's Soft Sugar Cookies is one of the recipes that saved the day for Dorene. See the recipe on page 127.

Eric R. Liscinsky
Damascus, Maryland

As many of you did, I grew up on my mother's home baked treats, especially her chocolate chip cookies. As a boy, I was always drawn to the "special" cookie tin. After a day of baking several dozen chocolate chip cookies my mother would try to hide the tin, which held about 6 or 7 dozen cookies. These were soft to start with and would cool to a firm and then crunchy cookie. They were great when hot as well as after they cooled. And "dunkable" was an understatement. It's why I became a "dunker." It became a contest between her and me to see if she could hide the tin without me finding it. I believe she loved the game, although she seemed frustrated each time I found it. There was no limit to her ingenuity and my tenacity.

As an example, I'll share with you my most memorable time. She had, as she did most times, spent the day making cookies for a holiday gathering. She hid the tin, and when I came home from school I could smell the chocolate chip cookies in the air. I dropped my things and (as usual) I began to beg her for an after-school treat. She said, "No," and that the cookies were for the coming holiday and that she hid the tin. She further said if I could find the tin I could have a few (dozen I hoped) for a "snack." The gauntlet had been thrown and I accepted it. What kid wouldn't? I ran through the house in minutes. Closets, cabinets, and the clothes drier, all the usual places. Then God must have given me inspiration and I went to the fireplace and looked up into the chimney. There it was!

As I became an adult I would still ask my mother for her cookies. Because she loved her little boy she would make them. You see, my wife, being very intelligent, didn't try her hand at making them, as she also thought them "the best she'd ever tasted." Once, I brought The Tin full of cookies to a beach vacation with my wife's family and the entire family proclaimed them "The Official Cookie" and my mother received many thanks and requests for future bakings. In fact any time I brought these cookies to parties, or gatherings of any kind, everyone asked where they came from and I never came home with any leftovers.

My mother is gone now, and no one has matched her chocolate chip cookies. This may be due to a nostalgic memory, but I don't think so. My sister-in-law comes the closest. And although I have picked up on some of my mother's baking skills, for many years I couldn't bring myself to make the chocolate chip cookies. I have the recipe card and wooden spoons she used. In fact, my wife has artistically arranged them on a grapevine wreath in our kitchen as inspiration to my efforts. I since, with the help of my sister-in-law, have tried baking them. Not bad—not the same, but not bad. I hope one day to match my mother's talent for baking, and inspire my children to bake "Grandma Helen's Chocolate Chip Cookies" too.

Grandma Helen's Chocolate Chip Cookies can be found on page 124.

Lynn Kopsie
Reading, Pennsylvania

In the 1950s my dear mother would bake cookies in quantity and store them in 5-gallon tin cans saved from potato chips. There were butter cut-outs, lions, stars, horses, ducks and "Ashtray" Sugar Cookies made with a ball of dough and pressed flat with a sugar-dipped, never used, glass bottom of an ashtray.

We three kids were made to feel welcome with sugar up to our armpits; we all grew up to be accomplished bakers and cooks.

Growing up on a country farm, Mom had the foresight to respect vitamins and minerals as a major part of nutrition and valued time proven remedies when money was scarce. This is where the favorite Christmas cookie began. Each approaching fall with the threat of the cold winds of winter beating our faces raw, Mom would save all fat taken from farm-raised geese and melt it to a liquid, clear, wonderful oil. When there was enough for a monster batch of cookies, the magic would begin.

Cup after cup of rolled oats would be mixed in with sugars, white and brown, raisins plump with the autumn juices of a harvest past, store-bought flour from 50-pound sacks, and that wonderful liquid magic that slipped from the measuring cup like melted glass. The mixing would begin by hand till every muscle kneaded love into every bite. The cookies baked in an old coal stove, surrounded by the memories of past Christmas baking. The black cast iron door opened to tray after tray of these goose fat cookies, baked to complete perfection.

We didn't need prompting to fill our pockets and stomachs with these treats as we ran out to play in the snow for hours on end, soaking wet to the marrow and never had even a sniffle. Thanks, Mom!

"Ashtray" Sugar Cookies can be found on page 132, and Old Fashioned Oatmeal Cookies are on page 134.

Angela Woodard
Hornlake, Missouri

This is the story of the first time I baked Christmas cookies with my daughter. She was 3 years old and I decided it was a time that she would remember since she was getting to be a "big girl" now. I purchased a kit to save on the prep time, because children are so impatient. The kit had everything to make 3 dozen of the most delicious cookies you can imagine, so we began mixing the kit ingredients.

My daughter wanted to know why she had to do all this mixing to make a cookie, since she was used to just getting her cookies out of the bag. I explained to her that it had to be dough before the cookies were actually cookies, so back to mixing we went. Finally we got to the point that we could start cutting out the cookies. I placed some of the dough on the counter and prepared to roll it out. My daughter beat me to the point and put her little hands in the dough. She said, "Mommy, I will make it flat." Well she did make it flat. It took her about 25 minutes but that was all right because she enjoyed it.

We started cutting out cookies into all the little Christmas shapes. Finally after about an hour we had the first batch ready to put in the oven. My daughter stood there with the widest eyes watching the dough cook and turn to a golden brown, and then as soon as they were ready we took them out and let them cool while we got the next batch ready to put in.

About 6 hours and 8 dozen cookies later we started to decorate them and get them ready to eat. I told her that we had to save some for Santa when he came to deliver all her toys on Christmas Eve and she looked me dead in the face and asked me, "Can't he have the bagged ones? I worked hard and want to keep these." I laughed, and then explained to her that Christmas is a time of sharing and giving and that we made these cookies so that we could share them and give them to others as well as have some for us. Her little brown eyes sparkled and she went to get a paper plate, then got one of each shape and gently placed them on the plate, and then looked right at me and said, "These are Santa's cookies. Do not let anyone touch them but Santa!"

She then helped me make up several gift bags of cookies. The next day we went to neighbors' houses and gave them the Christmas cookies we made. This has become a mother-daughter tradition since that day. Every year, my daughter says, "It's time to make Christmas cookies for the neighbors and Santa!"

Johanne Bezaire
Napanee, Ontario

For at least five generations my family has baked Speculaci every Christmas, using my great-grandmother's old tin cookie cutters (plus others we've all collected over the decades). Her family had emigrated from Alsace to Canada in the 1840s, when settlers had to clear great forests from land they hoped to farm. The recipe for the cookies is printed in a 1920s cookbook published by the women's association of the Brewster Congregational Church in Detroit, Michigan, to which city the family had moved in the 1880s.

When I was a little girl we decorated the cookies with coloured sugars, tiny candies and dragées. When my children were small I started to ice the little animals, birds, Christmas trees, bells and stars with a white glaze and then we all painted our fancies on them with vegetable colouring, adding coloured sugars and dragées for trim. If you start painting when the icing is still soft you get a water-colour effect, soft and impressionist; if you wait until the surface is hard the colours are crisper and clearer, more like enamel. We poke holes in some of the cookies before baking so they can hang on the kitchen Christmas tree. My grandchildren love these the best of all the Christmas treats.

When I was growing up in the '40s and '50s my family did a tremendous amount of baking before Christmas. My mother made Springerle, Pfeffernuesse and an icebox cookie bright with cherries; my father made his special shortbread and Stollen, and we all worked on the huge Christmas fruitcakes. Since then I've collected Scandinavian and German Christmas cookie recipes, and although I'm now diabetic, I still bake up a storm and pass the goodies to family and friends. But the one cookie we'd make, if we had to choose just one, would be my great-grandmother's Speculaci.

I still have blown glass ornaments from her collection and hang them on my parlour tree. When my own collection became too much for the largest tree I could find I started to buy two trees. Now the one in the parlour wears hundreds of delicate glass ornaments, while the kitchen tree has the unbreakables—fleets of little wooden ships, pewter representations of historic Kingston buildings, papier mâché fruits, feather birds, garlands of popcorn and cranberries, and of course the Speculaci menagerie, hung high so the dogs don't have Christmas early.

Johanne's vintage Speculaci recipe is found on page 121.

Karen Curtis
Spring, Texas

My favorite part of Christmas is the tradition of baking old-fashioned butter cookies. I can't remember a part of my childhood where I was not in Grandma's kitchen, baking and cooking right alongside in my own kid-size apron. Grandma has been gone for several years now. I have her old *Better Homes and Gardens* cookbook. It is full of handwritten recipes taped and glued in, along with her own notes on some recipes. The butter cookie recipe is one of the handwritten ones.

Although I'm sure I could make the cookies without ever looking at the recipe again, I always use Grandma's tattered cookbook and include my Grandma in my Christmas baking.

Index of Recipes

Recipes by Type

Bar Cookies

Biscotti

Breads

Candy

Recipes by Delivery Method

Hand Delivery

Visit us on the Web at:
http://www.christmascookiesareforgiving.com/

If you enjoyed this book, please post a review at your
favorite online bookstore today.

ABOUT THE AUTHORS

KRISTIN JOHNSON, an award-winning writer and a graduate of the University of Southern California Master of Professional Writing Program, has written about food for LivingRight.com and since her childhood is famous among her family and friends for baking Christmas cookies, particularly the family Nut Roll and German Christmas Cookies recipes. Her cookie-baking and her work on *Christmas Cookies Are for Giving* led to a feature article in The Desert Sun in January 2003. She published her first novel, *Butterfly Wings: A Love Story,* in August 2000 and her third book, *Ordinary Miracles: My Incredible Spiritual, Artistic and Scientific Journey,* a collaboration with two-time Nobel Prize nominee Sir Rupert A.L. Perrin, M.D. on his memoir, will be published by PublishAmerica in 2004. A produced playwright, she recently began working on her fourth and fifth books. She is a busy lady who also maintains PoemsForYou.com, a writing business that provides biographies in verse, or celebratory poems for all occasions. She's involved with her local chapter of Women In Film and the Palm Springs Branch of the National League of American Pen Women. She currently lives and writes in Palm Desert, California.

MIMI CUMMINS grew up baking cookies with her grandmother and is an avid cookbook reader and recipe tester. She learned professional baking while attending the University of San Diego, where she worked with the university pastry chef preparing desserts and baked goods for the campus restaurants and deli. As soon as she discovered the Internet, her interest naturally found an expression there. One of her first Web sites was dedicated to the legendary Christmas cookie recipes of her grandmother Evelyn. The site soon grew into the hugely popular Christmas-Cookies.com, the most comprehensive repository of Christmas cookie recipes on the Internet. Mimi's exploits on the web eventually led her to turn her web design hobby into a profession and she is now the Design Manager at Xenocast. She has designed Web sites for national chains and her work has garnered the attention of the US and Canadian news media. She lives and bakes in Quebec, Canada with her husband and three boys. This is her first book.

Notes

Notes

Published by:

Tyr Publishing is a small press promoting books of the highest quality in their genre.

To order:
To order additional copies of this book visit us online at
http://www.tyrpublishing.com/

Book design and cover design by:

Xenocast: Street Smart Media Solutions

Creative • Technologies • Marketing • Consulting

Visit us on the web at http://www.xenocast.com/